Writing for New Media

The Essential Guide to Writing for Interactive Media, CD-ROMs, and the Web

Andrew Bonime
Ken C. Pohlmann

John Wiley & Sons, Inc.

New York • Chichester • Weinheim • Brisbane • Singapore • Toronto

This text is printed on acid-free paper. ∞

Copyright © 1998 by Andrew Bonime and Ken C. Pohlmann
All rights reserved.
Published by John Wiley & Sons, Inc.
Published simultaneously in Canada.

This publication is designed to provide accurate and authoritative information in regard to the subject matter covered. It is sold with the understanding that the publisher is not engaged in rendering legal, accounting, or other professional services. If legal advice or other expert assistance is required, the services of a competent professional person should be sought.

Library of Congress Cataloging-in-Publication Data
Bonime, Andrew
    Writing for new media : the essential guide to writing for interactive media, CD-ROMs, and the Web / Andrew Bonime, Ken C. Pohlmann.
        p. cm.
    Includes index.
    ISBN 0-471-17030-5 (paper : alk. paper)
    1. Interactive multimedia—Authorship.   2. CD-ROMs.   3. World Wide Web (Information retrieval system)   I. Pohlmann, Ken C.   II. Title.
QA76.76.I59B65   1997
808'.066006—dc21   97-25193

Printed in the United States of America

10   9   8   7   6   5   4   3   2   1

Contents

Acknowledgments

As with any gestation and birth, the discomfort and pain of writing a book all becomes worth it when the offspring is brought into the world. Unlike offspring of the DNA variety, the book you are holding has many parents. Here they are:

My wife, Linda, saw me through the agony of facing the blank page by just being what she has always been to me and to everyone who knows her—a force for good. Ken Pohlmann, my co-author, started this whole thing rolling by asking me if I would like to "ruin a year of [my] life" to write a book. I have been a fan of Ken's writing ever since I first read his articles in *Stereo Review* many years ago. It is an honor to be working with him.

John Wright, our agent, is any writer's dream. His editorial skill and belief in this book from the beginning are the reasons it was published.

The editorial people at John Wiley have been terrific, and they have been highly supportive as well. P.J. Dempsey, who signed this book, and Chris Jackson, who edited it, were very helpful in shaping it early on. I also owe a debt of gratitude to Joanne Palmer, our managing editor, who not only made it more readable, but whose voluminous questions helped assure that the authors would not be the only people who understand the book.

The new media magicians at Imergy are owed my gratitude as well for providing an exciting laboratory to test out many of the ideas discussed in this book.

And definitely not least, I want to thank Ripley, my West Highland White Terrier, who dynamically responds to the user's actions, and may be the most interactive dog on the planet.

Andrew Bonime
New York, NY

Introduction

If you have thought about authoring a CD-ROM, creating a Web page, or writing interactive content for any of the new electronic media, this book is for you. If you write fiction or nonfiction for the print media and you've been asked to write an interactive article or an interactive story, you should read this book. If you are a student or teacher of composition or writing skills, you may have considered that interactive media require a writing skill that is as specialized as writing for theater or film; this book is also for you. Most businesses require traditional writing skills for corporate communication. The same businesses are also embracing interactive media for applications such as training, advertising, presentations, and creating sales material. In short, whether you are a student, teacher, professional author, or businessperson who writes, this book will help you to develop the skills needed for successful interactive writing using new electronic media.

Clearly, we have entered a new age as computer technology has changed our lives. Those of us who write have witnessed the utter obsolescence of the very symbol of professional writing—the typewriter. Instead, we write with personal computers and word processing software. Still, at least in the early stages of this revolution, the reader was not affected. If a book or magazine article was our end result, our means of production was irrelevant to the reader, who was not equipped with any new means of retrieving the information we had written. As long as we create printed pages, we can use a word processor, a typewriter, or a quill pen and parchment, without affecting our writing style or the reader's method of retrieval.

But we know that not all writing reaches the reader directly. Playwrights and screenwriters create characters and dramatic structure the same way a novelist does, but the end result must be translated through the interpretation of the director, actors, and technicians. This kind of writing is not done with a reader in mind, but rather as the blueprint for a *process*. For centuries, playwrights have written copious stage directions into their plays. They instruct performers, set designers, directors, and technicians in ways that the audience can only experience indirectly. Later, motion picture technology introduced its particular screenwriting variation into the writing process, and similarly it is the advent of computer technology that has today created interactive writing.

When film was in its infancy, early experimenters such as Thomas Edison had no idea that this new technology would evolve into an art form. Instead, they concentrated on its novel ability to capture motion. This is understandable; when any new technology is devised, people want to exploit what it fundamentally does. And what film did was show motion. The earliest arcade films were literally sequences of images showing, for example, a person sneezing. At first, filmmakers photographed their sequences from a single camera position. Soon they discovered that they could vary this and shoot close-ups, medium shots, and long shots. The art of editing was born, and with it, a new grammar for the new medium. Simultaneously, filmmakers discovered that the medium could be used to tell stories. The idea of cinematic drama was born.

Screenwriters now had to invent a new form of writing that used scenes and shots. They needed to invent types of montages and other techniques useful for telling cinematic stories. Most importantly, they invented ways to use the new medium to affect the viewer. They discovered that cutting two shots together created a sort of dialectic. They discovered that emotions could be evoked by the creative juxtaposition of images. Screenwriters discovered that the screenplay is very different from the film; screenwriting became a distinct form of writing. In the late 1960s film writing gained recognition as an academic subject and college courses appeared throughout the world. This new kind of grammar had become acknowledged and accepted.

Today, interactive media is enjoying similar recognition as the technology of CD-ROM and online communication take hold in our society. These technologies are no longer novelties—they are big business, and have even achieved artistic status. Increasingly, writers are called upon to exercise an understanding of the syntax and grammar of these new media that are as unique as those needed by screenwriters to successfully write for film. This book grew out of the demand for interactive writers and writers' need to understand the different demands and opportunities of the new media. Writers often ask us what they need to know to write for interactive media. They all ask the same questions: How much material can I put on a CD-ROM? I have an idea for a Web site—is it feasible? I've been asked to write an article for a CD-ROM encyclopedia; how do I do it?

These questions can generally be answered rather easily. More difficult are the underlying grammar and syntax needed to create good interactive media. While this knowledge tends to be nontechnical in nature, a certain understanding of technology is needed to grasp the impact of the task at hand. Returning to the film analogy, a screenwriter may not need to know much about the technology of film, but the screenwriter will benefit, for example, from the knowledge that a telephoto lens has the effect of compressing spatial relationships between foreground and distant objects. This knowledge better equips the screenwriter to visualize and write a scene, for example, in which the characters must look like they are running and not getting anywhere. In much the same way, a basic knowledge of new media technology is extremely helpful in writing for the interactive media.

Still, it is primarily the writer's craft that concerns us here, not interactive multimedia technology. If you are an interactive writer or want to become one, you do not need to know about the intricate workings of the computer code of a word processing program. When you first learned to drive a car, you probably didn't first master the inner workings of the internal combustion engine, but you did learn how to parallel park (well, at least sort of). This book follows the simple thesis that the technology is our car, and we're going to learn how to drive, and drive well. In other words, this is a book about writing for a new medium that happens to make use of interactive computer technology.

Most interactive works contain elements of multimedia. In multimedia, the writer can mix various types of visuals and audio with the text. The mix can vary tremendously. In some cases, text is the framework for the interactive title. Photographs, illustrations, animation, and video can be interspersed within the text and can be accessed at the user's discretion. In other cases, the entire framework is presented using still images, animation, and audio while the text itself is supplemental. No matter what the format, all of these titles must be written by someone who understands the nature of interactivity.

Sometimes called *interactive media, multimedia,* or *new media,* these technology-based forms of information and entertainment delivery require an entirely new approach to writing because interactive media present their content in a nonlinear fashion. It is linear writing in which we are traditionally educated. Traditional writing skill requires a grammar based on a linear logic flow to structure our ideas. Interactive writing skills require that we create an architecture that allows and encourages structural manipulation by the reader. Much of the writing within that structure may possess a linear integrity, but the overall content should be accessible in any order at the command of the reader. The writer can no longer assume that the reader has the foundation information on which successive information is to be based. In fact, the writer cannot assume that the reader will access the information in any particular order. Thus, the interactive writer must work with an entirely new paradigm in which information, which would otherwise depend on previous knowledge, can be conveyed nonlinearly. This requires a new grammar and a new set of tools for the writer.

In a limited sense, there already exist many forms of writing that fit this definition of nonlinearity: Dictionaries, encyclopedias, and directories all present small chunks of information in reader-determined order. A person looking up *zymurgy* in a dictionary need not already know the meaning of *aardvark.* But interactive media goes much further. As we shall see, an interactive book on the French Revolution should be written so that the linear description of historical events may be read out of order. In this way, the reader may skip around yet depart with information that was both efficiently and coherently presented.

For example, let's say that you know nothing about the French Revolution and you want to follow the chain of events. You may soon feel overwhelmed by the number of politicians, militarists, and members of the royal family you need to track. It would be helpful if you could pause your linear investigation of the events to learn about Robespierre, then return to the linear story; you'd be better equipped to follow the narrative. But suppose you know all about Robespierre and you just want to follow the historical time line. You'd have that option as well. The writer need not be concerned with every reader's level of familiarity with the material or reason for studying the material. With a nonlinear architecture, each user can take the path most appropriate for his or her personal knowledge base, interest, and experience.

According to Marshall McLuhan, media are either hot or cool. Hot media supply the recipient with enough information to form a fully developed image in his or her mind. Cool media force the recipient to fill in some of the information. For example, a photograph is hot compared to a cartoon, which is cool.

But McLuhan never addressed interactive media, and so he was unable to comment on the dynamic flow of information back and forth from content to user. Interactivity adds a new dimension to the hot/cool spectrum of McLuhan by infusing even the coolest of media with the ability to be heated up by the user.

In this book, we intend to give both novice and seasoned linear writers a firm grasp of the fundamental principles of writing for interactive media, without tying these principles to a specific technology. As technology advances, new methods of information delivery will undoubtedly appear, but there will always be a fundamental need for organization and presentation of information and storytelling. Whether using a mouse or placing a finger on a touch screen, the reader will always choose the information to be accessed, and that information must be organized and presented according to a well-defined structure and syntax that is appropriate for the medium. We hope that this book will successfully introduce you to the craft of interactive writing, and that this understanding will be useful today and for a long time to come.

Part One

What Is Interactive Writing?

1

What Is Interactivity?

Thank you for calling American Amalgamated Industries. If you wish to speak to someone in customer service, press the number one followed by the pound sign on your telephone keypad. . . .

—Automated telephone answering service

Everyday Interactivity

Interactivity is such a simple concept that it should be very easy to explain, yet it continues to confound many people. So let's start out with a simple definition: Interactivity is the property of any medium that responds dynamically to user control.

Of course, this is one of those definitions that sometimes creates more confusion than it eliminates. The reason it adds to the confusion is that we generally think of interactivity as a new concept and in particular something associated with technology. But our definition doesn't mention either newness or technology.

In fact, interactivity is not new at all and may or may not have anything to do with technology. A horse responds to its rider's heels kicking its sides and the reins being tugged in one direction or the other. The horse turns left as the rider pulls the reins to the left. In other words, a rider on a horse forms an interactive system. Similarly, to a driver, a car is an interactive system; we say that a car is an interactive transportation device because it responds to the driver's control. In terms of our definition of interactivity, the control of the user (pulling the reins or turning the steering wheel) produces an action (altering the course of the horse or car) as a direct response. We may glance at the speedometer on the car's dashboard and see that we need to slow down a bit. In this case we and the car are involved in dynamic response to each other—fitting our definition of interactivity even better.

Definition aside, most people wouldn't conclude that they were riding in an "interactive car." Perhaps that is because the word *interactive* is usually applied to devices and activities that provide some sort of communication service. Let's consider some everyday devices and see if they are indeed interactive, and if so, just how interactive they are.

At first glance, the telephone is a classic interactive device: You punch in a number and it establishes a connection to another telephone corresponding to that number; the phone on the other end starts to ring (or chirp or buzz). Up until this point the telephone has met most of the criteria of our definition: It responded to user input because it located and engaged another device through which it could communicate. But in our definition the action must respond "*dynamically* to the user's control." This requirement is met only when a user on the other end picks up the telephone to open a communication channel and begins talking. When that oral communication is initiated, the action (communication) becomes dynamic because the user responds dynamically to the communication from the other end and vice versa. A telephone fits our definition of an interactive medium only when communication is actually established.

Interactive TV

There is much discussion today about the concept of interactive television. But according to our definition, isn't conventional television already interactive? Let's see: When we press the On button the television turns on, and we can change channels by pressing buttons on the remote control. It seems that television meets the criteria. If we are "channel surfing" and we see something that interests us, we stop surfing and watch in a non-interactive mode for awhile. Then, when a commercial comes on, we hit the Mute button. All of this is essentially dynamic because our actions control the delivery of information which in turn influences our further actions.

However, aside from controlling the flow of information in response to our desire to watch/not watch, listen/not listen, or stay with/change the current channel, television lacks the dynamic level of interaction we have with the telephone. We conclude that conventional television is somewhat interactive. This demonstrates that interactivity exists in varying degrees.

Commercial broadcast television, for example, is more interactive than what is broadcast in a static, closed-circuit security system.

However, a truly interactive television system should be more interactive than forms of television with which we are most familiar. Let's suppose that you're watching a television show about wild game in Tanzania and you are curious about some exotic animals that appear on the screen. Suppose you could use your remote control to move a cursor on the screen over one of the animals and click a button to find out that the exotic animals are in fact wildebeests. Suppose you could point to the word *wildebeest* and get more information about it, including the fact that wildebeests live on the Serengeti Plain in Africa. Now you want to know more about the Serengeti Plain, so you point to the word *Serengeti*, which is in a box on your screen. When you click on it, a map appears with the Serengeti region highlighted. Now that the map is on your screen, you start selecting other geographic spots you find interesting. You finish by selecting Tell Me More from a menu, and you get a list of other television shows on similar topics. You further request that a book called *Animals of the Serengeti* be charged to your credit card and shipped to your home address. By the time you're through, beginning by simply watching a show on one topic, you've followed your interests through a series of links to other topics and even performed a financial transaction based on this information.

What's truly dynamic about this is that as you jumped from link to link, you were motivated by each link to seek out another in the chain. In this case, the new information dynamically affected the way you used your interactive control. This type of television is much more interactive than traditional television because it responds *dynamically* to your actions.

Are Books and Magazines Interactive?

It is unlikely that many people intentionally read the last page of a mystery novel first. In fact, most novels are intended to be read from the beginning straight through to the end. But the same cannot be said for dictionaries and encyclopedias and, in fact, most magazines and newspapers. You find what you want to read in these publications by looking through the table of contents or index, or by flipping the pages to find articles of interest to you. You are often instructed to turn to a certain page to continue reading an article. Sidebars often present additional information that is related to the main article. This type of dynamic action-and-response could certainly be deemed interactive because the printed material instructs readers how to locate information. Readers, in turn, decide whether to follow these instructions, depending on their interest. Readers may, for example, decide not to turn to a certain page if they no longer want to continue reading the article. Or readers may notice some other article that distracts them from the original one.

Reference books have varying degrees of interactivity. Some books must be read more or less in chapter order so that the reader can comprehend successive chapters based on foundational information. Other reference works require no such linear approach. The book you are currently reading falls somewhere in between: You can read any chapter without having to read those that precede it, but in some chapters, references and concepts refer to earlier chapters. Certain chapters are self-contained and make almost no reference to any other part of the book, while others relate more or less directly or indirectly to other chapters. So, as with television, printed material can have varying degrees of interactivity.

Books and magazines may be interactive, but they are low tech media. They provide information, but we must look it up. Books may contain indexes and tables of contents, but we must manually locate the information by turning pages, and that takes time. Laziness aside, time is an important factor in information retrieval. Think back to your days as a third grader: Do you remember raising your hand and asking your teacher to define a particular word? The teacher probably said, "Look it up in the dictionary." You might remember feeling vaguely let down. Not that looking up the word was such a difficult task, but you wanted the definition immediately. The short time it took to walk over to the massive classroom dictionary, leaf through the pages, and locate the word was not a major impediment, but the delay in information gratification was annoying.

The desire for instant information gratification stays with us through adulthood. This is because, at least in part, our level of curiosity is directly linked to our ability to comprehend and retain information. The more timely the arrival of information is to our highest level of curiosity, the more the information is likely to provide satisfaction as the entire process reaches what psychologists call "closure." To put it another way, the shorter the time period between the question and the answer, the more satisfying the process, and the greater the likelihood the information will be retained.

This is where computers have revolutionized the process of accessing information. By automating the aspects of navigating a database and finding desired information, computers help minimize the time between questions and answers. In addition, they provide the ability to customize the very structure of information according to the user's desires.

Interactivity and the New Media

Throughout this book, we will consider how to author interactive materials for computers, but for now it's important to understand that when we say "computers" we don't necessarily mean those putty-colored appliances on our desks. Computers come in all shapes and sizes, and they are omnipresent. There are computers in your car, in your television, and perhaps in your thermostat. Even your wristwatch is likely to contain a computer. Even if you have no computer in your home (nearly impossible today), your telephone is connected to a network of computers.

Whatever the guise of the computer, computer-driven versions of traditional media are collectively called *new media* or *interactive media*. If audio, video, or animation is linked to the text, they are often called *multimedia*. Computers can automate tasks we used to do manually but whose slowness frustrated our need for instant information gratification. Computers also do things previously impossible. Computers can

- Look things up for us
- Navigate for us ("Please turn to page . . .")
- Link words to other words
- Remember where we were and take us back there
- Play audio, video, and animation
- Organize and present information according to a nonlinear structure

While interactivity has always existed in other media to some degree or another, it is the computer that has brought interactivity to its prime. To understand why this is true, we must understand the difference between a book and its computer counterpart (or *ebook*). For purposes of this discussion, let's assume that when we say "book" we mean all traditional print material ranging from novels to telephone directories, from gum wrappers to packing slips, from billboards to soda cans.

Books: Pros and Cons

Consider the book in your hands. It is a self-contained, inert system. It requires no playback device. You read it by simply looking at it. When parts of it are hidden, you move the obstructions out of the way by turning pages. The pages are numbered and you navigate by virtue of your understanding of the numbering system. If you want to find something in a book, you either leaf through its pages and scan the text for the words or phrases that indicate the subject of interest, or you use a table of contents or index that assigns a number to the page on which the information is located. Once you know the page number, you look at the top or bottom of the pages where the page numbers are located and find the page you're looking for. If the book has illustrations, there are usually numbers assigned to them; the text uses the numbers to link the image to the text. If you are using a reference work like a dictionary, encyclopedia, or telephone directory, you use your knowledge of the alphabet to locate your subject. Of course, if the subject you are looking for is more conceptual than specific, it might not be tied to a particular word, so it may be more difficult to locate. All of this may seem like a statement of the obvious, but it points up one thing: A book efficiently provides information, but does very little to help us access the information.

Still, let's not be too harsh on the venerable scion of Gutenberg's genius. Books printed on paper are incredibly efficient devices, and print publishing will endure for many years to come. There are some very good reasons for this:

Books are tactile.   You hold a book in your hand and you can turn to any page, always maintaining complete control over it. A book is terrific for browsing. When you look at a book in a bookstore or library, you can flip through the pages and almost immediately get a sense of what is contained within its covers.

Books are personal.   Because no device, electronic or otherwise, comes between the book and the reader (except, perhaps, for corrective lenses), the relationship is direct and intimate. There's nothing better than snuggling up with a book on a rainy day or before falling asleep in bed.

Books travel well.   With paperback versions of dictionaries, language phrase books and other travel books, and even encyclopedias, the reader can bring a book directly to the location where it can best be used. On subways and buses everywhere, commuters read newspapers and books. Similarly, you find newsstands and bookstores in every airport and train station.

Property	Books	Ebooks
Tactile	Yes	No
Random access	Yes/No (Books can be randomly accessed, but many are designed for sequential access.)	Yes
Text	Yes	Yes
Pictures	Yes	Yes
Audio	No	Yes
Video	No	Yes
Search	No	Yes
Hyperlinking	No	Yes
Portable	Yes	Yes/No (Media is usually portable, but it may require nonportable equipment to access it.)
Customizable	No	Yes
Information transfer	Photocopy	Digital (Digital information can be copied and pasted into any other document and sent to any other digital device in the world instantly).

Books present themselves.   A large book on art may function as much like a piece of furniture as it does a work of reference. You can enjoy the color reproductions in an art book or the photographs in a travel book in a random manner and just let the contents inspire you. Also, any book's cover art forms part of its unique identity.

Computers make books better by eliminating some of their drawbacks. But computers may also make books worse by eliminating some of their positive features. The computer's ability to locate information, navigate through it, link up concepts, and add multimedia eliminates many inherent drawbacks of books. On the other hand, with computer-driven media, at least with present authoring methods, direct contact and intimacy with the actual information is lost. The chart on page 15 summarizes the properties of books and computer-driven media, showing some pros and cons.

The best examples of interactive media are those in which the book's drawbacks are improved but its advantages are not harmed. Because of the nature of interactive media this ideal is not easy to achieve, but as we shall see it is not an impossible task, either.

Summary

We defined interactivity as the property of any action that responds dynamically to user control. As a basic concept, interactivity has been with us for a long time: Telephones and television provide a degree of interactivity. Computers greatly enhance the power of interactivity because they give us the ability to interact with text, images, audio, and video in ways that often improve on the functionality of a paper book. Paper books are efficient storage devices but do not provide optimal access. When properly authored, new media should offer efficient access and storage, increase interactivity, and constructively add functionality with multimedia elements.

2

Books and Ebooks

Computer science only indicates the retrospective omnipotence of our technologies. In other words, an infinite capacity to process data (but only data— i.e., the already given) and in no sense a new vision.

—Jean Baudrillard, French semiologist

From Books to Bits

To understand how a book becomes interactive, we need to know a little about how computers work. To put it simply: Computers can add, but they can't read. Computers have no capability whatsoever of dealing directly with letters, words, punctuation, or anything remotely resembling language as we know it. Computers only deal with numbers. Fundamentally, they can add numbers and they can compare numbers. They can tell whether one number is the same as, greater than, or less than another number. Building on these basics, they can perform complex numerical operations with incredible speed, thus processing tremendous amounts of numeric information in a very short time.

If computers can only deal with numbers, how can they be of use to writers? Obviously, computers can deal with letters, words, and punctuation, but they do it indirectly. For computers to be able to handle text, the text must first be converted to numbers. When we type the letter *a* on a computer keyboard, the computer actually processes the character as a string of binary values: 1100001. This is done invisibly to the user. We rarely have to know anything about this process. Each character is stored according to a universally standardized code that assigns a number to every letter, numeric figure, punctuation mark, and symbol. This code is called *ASCII* (pronounced ASK-ee), which stands for American Standard Code for Information Interchange.

If we want the computer to recognize text that already exists as hard-copy print, we must convert it into a machine-readable form using a scanner, actually a kind of photocopying machine, that sends an image of the page to the computer instead of to paper. Once in the computer, the image of the page is represented by numbers that the computer can use to create a picture of the page on the screen. At this point, the computer does not know that the picture of the page has letters on it. (The computer sees this page as if it were any photograph or drawing.) To convert the text to numbers representing each individual character, a program called an Optical Character Recognition (OCR) program is used to look at the picture, find the image of each letter, and assign its proper code.

Pictures, audio, and video are also translated into numbers. The main difference is that there is no single standard code for them, and there exist different codes for representing them as numbers. For example, an image may be represented as a JPEG or GIF file. Whatever code is used for text, pictures, audio, or video, they are all translated into numbers. This process is called *digitizing*. When these elements exist in a form that the computer can use, we say they are in *digital form*. Because computers can only understand two digits, 1 and 0, the representation is said to be *binary*. Instead of saying *BInary digiT*, we say *bit*. If a bit can only be a 1 or 0, its ability to represent larger numbers is quite limited unless it is put, along with other bits, into a group. Computers tend to deal with groups of eight bits at a time. These groups of eight bits are called *bytes*.

Good news: Writers don't need to understand any of this. As a writer, all you need to know is that

- Computers can process numbers in many different ways, and can similarly process text that has been converted to numbers.
- Text, pictures, audio, and video all must be converted to digital form to enable the computer to use it.

When you consider that Macintosh computers, PCs, handheld devices, online systems, and all the products that use computer technology to deliver text or multimedia information all use different systems, it becomes apparent that perhaps the only thing they all have in common is that they all manipulate information in digital form. In other words, the only concept we need to understand from the writer's point of view is that the new media are all digital media.

The Elements of Interactivity and Ebooks

Now that we have begun to focus on the modern view of interactivity as a function of computers and their related technology, let's look at the specific elements that make an ebook interactive. We will use the word *ebook* to describe a digital title and differentiate it from a paper book. Also, we should note that an ebook can describe any kind of electronic book, ranging from a CD-ROM title to an online interactive database, including the World Wide Web (two technologies that we'll describe in Chapter 21).

Basic Navigation

The first thing that most computers must be able to do with digital media is display it. Computers often use a screen to display visual information such as text, pictures, and video. Unlike a book, an ebook cannot be directly touched or leafed through. So a computer must first be able to accomplish what a book already does: It must provide a way for the user to move through the information. Computers have many options for this. They can present the pages in a book metaphor, showing images of actual pages on the screen, as shown in Figure 2.1. Another way is to present the text as if it were on one continuous page and the screen were a window onto a section of it. The user would scroll from top to bottom to read it (or back up if necessary).

This takes care of sequential access, but it is hardly an improvement over books that can be accessed both sequentially (when a reader turns each page in order) or nonsequentially (when she looks for specific information). Before we can improve on the book, we must first be able to provide means to accomplish what every book can already do. Since we cannot physically turn pages in an ebook, we must have other methods of getting around. Computers allow many types of access. Here are the most basic ways you can navigate through an ebook:

- Go to a "page" by typing in or selecting the page number.
- Go to a subject by typing in or selecting the heading.
- Scroll through the text or turn the page.

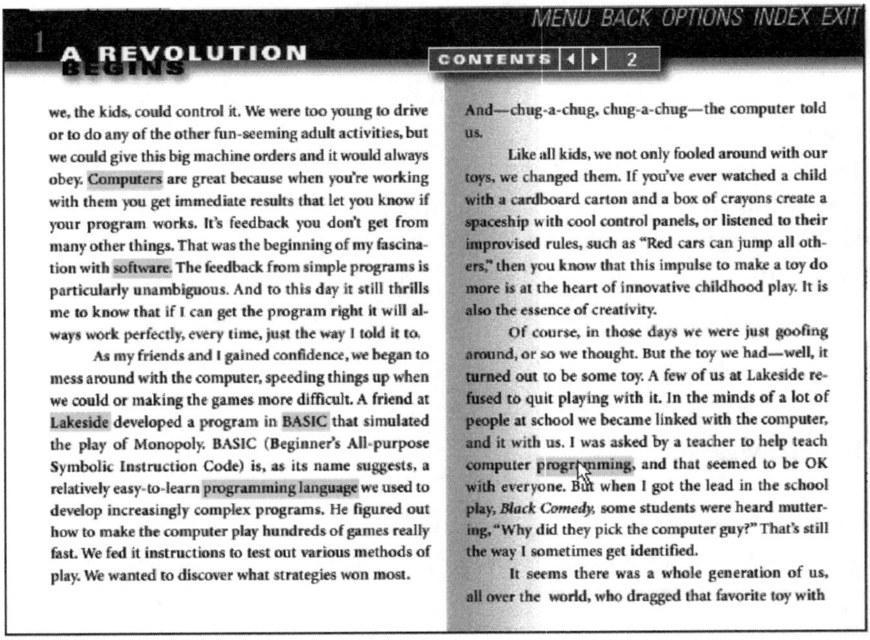

we, the kids, could control it. We were too young to drive or to do any of the other fun-seeming adult activities, but we could give this big machine orders and it would always obey. Computers are great because when you're working with them you get immediate results that let you know if your program works. It's feedback you don't get from many other things. That was the beginning of my fascination with software. The feedback from simple programs is particularly unambiguous. And to this day it still thrills me to know that if I can get the program right it will always work perfectly, every time, just the way I told it to.

As my friends and I gained confidence, we began to mess around with the computer, speeding things up when we could or making the games more difficult. A friend at Lakeside developed a program in BASIC that simulated the play of Monopoly. BASIC (Beginner's All-purpose Symbolic Instruction Code) is, as its name suggests, a relatively easy-to-learn programming language we used to develop increasingly complex programs. He figured out how to make the computer play hundreds of games really fast. We fed it instructions to test out various methods of play. We wanted to discover what strategies won most.

And—chug-a-chug, chug-a-chug—the computer told us.

Like all kids, we not only fooled around with our toys, we changed them. If you've ever watched a child with a cardboard carton and a box of crayons create a spaceship with cool control panels, or listened to their improvised rules, such as "Red cars can jump all others," then you know that this impulse to make a toy do more is at the heart of innovative childhood play. It is also the essence of creativity.

Of course, in those days we were just goofing around, or so we thought. But the toy we had—well, it turned out to be some toy. A few of us at Lakeside refused to quit playing with it. In the minds of a lot of people at school we became linked with the computer, and it with us. I was asked by a teacher to help teach computer programming, and that seemed to be OK with everyone. But when I got the lead in the school play, *Black Comedy*, some students were heard muttering, "Why did they pick the computer guy?" That's still the way I sometimes get identified.

It seems there was a whole generation of us, all over the world, who dragged that favorite toy with

Figure 2.1 Screen from *The Road Ahead*, a CD-ROM title packaged with the book by Bill Gates. It uses the metaphor of a set of pages from a real book. Even the 3-D shading on the right page suggests a real book. (*Screen shot reprinted with permission from Microsoft Corporation.*)

It is possible to retain much of the feel of a paper book by displaying pages that can be turned. Some ebooks even play the sound of a page turning as you flip it over. But if this were all that computers could do, there'd be little point to the exercise. However, computers offer extremely powerful ways to access information that go far beyond anything possible with a paper book.

Hyperlinking

Computers allow us to link any point in our ebook with any other point. For example, we can click on a word with our mouse and jump to related information located in another part of our ebook. The places on which we can click are called *hot spots* or *links*. A hot spot can be a word or phrase, a picture or graphic design, or part of a picture or a graphic design. A hot spot can be linked to text elsewhere in the ebook, or it can trigger playback of an audio or video clip, among many other things. This is called *hyperlinking*. Hyperlinking was formerly called *hypertext* because it originally did not involve multimedia. But as computers became more powerful, the ability to link text to audio, video, and pictures expanded their capability so that it is now called *hypermedia* or simply hyperlinking.

In Chapter 4 we shall see how hyperlinking opens up entirely new ways of presenting information in a nonlinear fashion. But for now, let's simply consider hyperlinking in terms of navigation. In a book there is generally a table of contents—a list of parts, chapters, and section headings with beginning page numbers assigned to each. In a magazine, the contents contains a list of features and article titles. The reader turns to the appropriate page to find the desired entry. The same is true of the book's index.

Through hyperlinking, a new navigational system can be implemented that automates the task of locating information in an ebook. We can present the table of contents as the first page on our screen and limit it to just part headings, as shown in Figure 2.2. This presents the main topic areas to the user (now that we're using digital media, *the reader* has become *the user* to denote an interactive relationship with the media). The user can point to the desired section and hyperlink to a new page that displays a listing of the chapters in that section. From here, the user can click on the chapter title and hyperlink to its text. This process is sometimes known as *drilling down* into the information structure. The advantage of this type of navigation is that it presents a neatly organized hierarchy of information to the user. It creates a more direct path to the desired information that is more efficient than looking through either the whole book or the complete chapter listing.

One of the problems with hyperlinking as a navigational tool is that it is easy to get lost within layers of hyperlinked locations as you skip from section to section. To make this all manageable, it has become an almost standard practice in interactive media to put a link back to the user's previous location and a link back to the beginning of the section on every screen or in a menu at a consistent location throughout the ebook. Usually this takes the form of a graphic representation of a button labeled Back or Main.

Aside from the ease and speed of locating information, hyperlinking has other advantages for both the user and the writer. It eliminates one of the most annoying aspects of using reference material: cross-references. Instead of using the conventions "See . . ." or "Turn to page . . .", the text

Feb. 8-10, 1997

PRINT SLATE | SLATE HELP | Contents by PAGE NUMBER DATE |

10. the dismal scientist
Vulgar Keynesians by Paul Krugman
A penny spent is not a penny earned?

11. it seems to me ...
The Cubist Republican by Herbert Stein
What Gertrude Stein and I share--beyond a last name.

12. strange bedfellow NEW
The Conservative Collapse by Jacob Weisberg
No ideas. No leaders. How did the Republican Party reach this point so quickly?

13. white house confidential NEW
I Had Coffee With Clinton by James J. Cramer
The inside story of those notorious White House

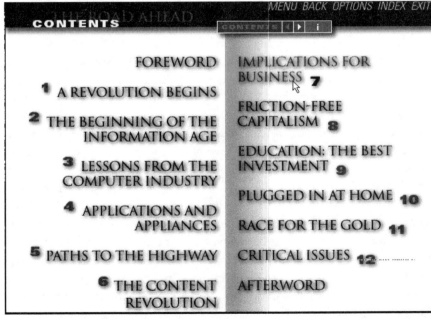

MENU BACK OPTIONS INDEX EXIT

CONTENTS   CONTENTS ◀ ▶ i

FOREWORD   IMPLICATIONS FOR
                 BUSINESS 7
1 A REVOLUTION BEGINS
                 FRICTION-FREE
2 THE BEGINNING OF THE   CAPITALISM 8
  INFORMATION AGE
                 EDUCATION: THE BEST
3 LESSONS FROM THE   INVESTMENT 9
  COMPUTER INDUSTRY
                 PLUGGED IN AT HOME 10
4 APPLICATIONS AND
  APPLIANCES   RACE FOR THE GOLD 11

5 PATHS TO THE HIGHWAY CRITICAL ISSUES 12

6 THE CONTENT   AFTERWORD
  REVOLUTION

Figure 2.2 (*Top*) The main menu screen from Slate on the Microsoft Network. Every article's title is hyperlinked to the actual article.

(*Bottom*) The table of contents from *The Road Ahead* by Bill Gates. Users simply click on a chapter heading and the title instantly puts the first page of that chapter on the screen. (*Screen shot reprinted with permission from Microsoft Corporation.*)

is simply identified so the user can jump to the cross-referenced text, or play the linked video or audio. In addition, the writer can dispense with definitions, elaborations, explanations, or much of the exposition by simply linking words and letting the user choose when and if further elaboration is needed. This can streamline the text, and it avoids disruptive side trips from the writer's main ideas. The techniques for using hyperlinks form a crucial aspect of interactive grammar, and we will explore this subject in much more depth in Chapters 11 through 14.

Searching

Probably the single most powerful thing a computer can do for an ebook user is to locate words or phrases within large volumes of text. Computers really can find the verbal equivalent of a needle in a haystack. In a traditional book, we are dependent on the index to locate the fundamental units of ideas within a larger text. Indexes are generally created by people who meticulously go through the text to find key words and phrases and prepare an alphabetical list with page numbers to refer the reader to their location within the text. The people who do this may use a computer to aid them, but they make judgments that determine what gets indexed and what does not. This can be a problem for the reader who may want to locate something the indexer has determined is not worthy of inclusion or simply has overlooked.

A computer search program makes no such judgments and makes no mistakes. Every word in the text can be located, except such common words as *a*, *the*, and *and*. The user can locate every occurrence of a useful word throughout a text.

Searching makes a phenomenal impact on information structure because it can create custom structures to suit the user's purpose. For example, let's consider an almanac. Editors of a paper almanac structure the information according to logical categories. They may present a list of all the countries in the world and give statistics on population, type of government, exports, and so on. They may choose to supplement this list with groupings, such as countries that export petroleum. But the reader may want to know all of the countries that export dairy products. With a computer, the user could search for the phrase *dairy products* and locate all relevant countries. This produces a custom list that the writers and editors never envisioned when they put together the almanac. When you consider online searching, an entirely new world of information begins to materialize. Imagine searching for *DNA* on the Internet. The results of that search represent not just one book, or even just one source of information about DNA, but potentially the entire universe of information on the topic. The user has created a personal compendium of customized information, in effect creating a book that never before existed.

But this brings up a potential problem: Is there such a thing as too much information? Suppose that when you searched for DNA, you were only interested in DNA as it relates to its use in forensics. If you simply searched for *DNA* or *forensic*, you may have ended up with too many articles to read, and you still may not have found what you were looking for. You could then use a *Boolean search* (named for George Boole, the inventor of Boolean algebra and its logical system). Boolean searches allow you to use words called *delimiters* such as *and, not,* and *or*. Using these delimiters, you can search for *DNA and forensic*. This would locate only those parts of the text or only those articles that contain both words, *DNA* and *forensic*, in the same article. You could search for *DNA or forensic*, and you would find all locations where either term existed, yielding all articles containing the term *DNA* and all articles containing the term *forensic*, but not necessarily containing both terms in the same article. This would produce many more results than *DNA and forensic* because there are many more articles that use one of the two words. Of course the yield of this search would include all the articles that contained both words.

Sometimes the term you want to find is cited in a context you don't want. Again, if you were to search for *DNA*, you might get too many citations about a major popular forensic usage. So, in this situation you might search for *DNA not O. J. Simpson*.

Searching can get so complex that it can become an art form. For example, you might search for *DNA and forensic not O. J. Simpson*. But the more complex searching techniques are mostly used by academics and researchers who use computer technology to locate research material on a regular basis. Interactive writers need be concerned only with the broadest of the following concepts:

- Searching can be used to locate a word or phrase within a large amount of online material encompassing many different publications located on computers all over the world.

- Searching can use the words and, not, and or to delimit the search to include other terms (and), exclude other terms (not), or supplement the search with other terms (or).

All searching is performed by a type of computer program called a *search engine.* It is important to realize that not all search engines are the same. Some are more powerful than others, some search general topics and others search only specific topics, some offer more features than others (such as Boolean search capability), some only search headings and some search all the text, and some even allow the user to specify the proximity of one search term to another in the text. Some search engines produce lists of articles by the name of each article's heading. Others take you directly to the part of the article where the search terms are mentioned, and they may even display the text with the search term highlighted.

Modern search engines can be so powerful that they can search for concepts rather than look for exact word matches. If you wanted to search for all information about AIDS in a medical text or online database, you would only find references that contained the actual acronym AIDS. But before 1983, although the condition was known, it was not known as AIDS; therefore, no references prior to this year would appear in your search. Likewise, if you wanted to search a geography text for Beijing, anything that appeared before 1980, when the city was called Peking, wouldn't show up. Topic or concept searches can find these concepts because experts in the appropriate subject matter create topic lists that contain words that the search engine looks for when any one of the words on the list is requested. A topic list for AIDS might include AIDS, HIV, autoimmune, and other related terms. So, if you searched for AIDS with a concept search engine, all articles containing any of the words on the list would show up even though they might not contain the actual acronym AIDS.

Search results can be weighted so that articles containing the search term can be ranked according to the probability that they actually contain what you are looking for. This means that the first results on the search result list are more likely to be relevant than those further down on the list. This can be accomplished because the search engine takes into account the number of times the search terms are mentioned in each article and the proximity each term has to the others. There are even advanced search engines that can search images so that you could ask for "all images predominantly yellow" or "all photographs of a sunset." This is just an example of how far the technology has come and a hint of where it is going.

Summary

Ebooks are any kind of electronic book in which information is stored and accessed digitally. This format provides the advantage of navigation. Hyperlinked materials allow users to move quickly from element to element, in effect creating a customized sequence of presentation. Electronic storage also allows the use of powerful search engines, computer programs that locate words or groups of words in a text. Using search engines, users can efficiently locate both very general or very specific information.

3

Intrinsic Interactivity: Some Media Are Already Interactive

The medium is the message. This is merely to say that the personal and social consequences of any medium—that is, of any extension of ourselves—result from the new scale that is introduced into our affairs by each extension of ourselves, or by any new technology.

—Marshall McLuhan

A Solution in Search of a Problem

Long ago, books replaced papyrus and parchment scrolls as the dominant information carrier. Books represented a great improvement because they can present information in a nonlinear form. Specifically, it is easier to access any page in a book directly than to wind through a parchment scroll. Paper books clearly demonstrate that interactivity is not new to the computer age, and in fact they rank among the best technologies ever invented.

Technology always works best when it is applied to a problem rather than as an end unto itself. Unfortunately, as many critics have pointed out, too often the new media seem to employ technology more to show it off than to serve the content. To avoid the pitfall of trying to fit interactivity into situations where it does not belong, it is useful to examine existing traditional media and see if we can identify some of the specific drawbacks that might benefit from the application of interactive technology.

How Interactivity Stems from Content

All media are subservient to their content. This may seem to be at odds with Marshall McLuhan's famous observation that the medium is the message, but that statement may have been more an observation of the (undesired) impact of technology on content than a statement of the (desired) principles to be followed. Unfortunately McLuhan's observation may still be true of interactive media because there are many examples of interactive material in which the content is less important than the fact that it is interactive. This is probably a result of the newness of the media, which motivates many of its creators to show off the technology. In fact, this follows the same historical developmental path followed by cinema, in which early films were nothing more than demonstrations of the technology of motion capture and reproduction.

However, good uses of interactivity ultimately stem from the relationship of the media to the content. Let's consider a few examples of traditional media to see how their content presents problems that can be solved by the application of interactivity.

The Talmud, Maps, and the Rosetta Stone

Before content can be interactive it must be nonlinear. If users are going to interact with content, they certainly will need to interact with it without regard to any particular order. History provides us with several examples of nonlinear content that might have become fully interactive if the technology had existed at the time.

Versions of the Talmud, the codification of Jewish civil and religious laws, present an interesting example of a neat solution to a content problem. The Talmud consists of a code of laws called the *Mishna*, and scholarly commentaries on these laws called the *Gemara*. Figure 3.1 shows a page of the Talmud in its original mixture of Hebrew and Aramaic. Rather than print the Mishna with footnotes or cross-references to the Gemara, which would have followed in a linear fashion, it was printed with the Mishna in the center of the page and the Gemara surrounding it. In this way, the sections of the commentary could be placed closest to the parts of the laws to which they referred. The value of the Talmud is greater than either the code of laws or the commentaries on them because the Mishna and the Gemara interact with each other, adding the unique dimension of integrated, interactive content.

Figure 3.1 This page from the Talmud shows the Mishna (the code of laws) in the center, with the Gemara (the commentaries on these laws) surrounding it. By placing the commentaries in proximity to the actual laws, the reader is able to participate in the interactive experience of relating content to its hyperlinked reference.

If we were to do the same thing with the U.S. Constitution, we might include in the outer ring all of the Supreme Court decisions interpreting each constitutional article, as shown in Figure 3.2. But obviously we'd have to use either very small type or a very large page, because there

The Constitution of the United States

PREAMBLE

We, the people of the United States, in order to form a more perfect Union, establish justice, insure domestic tranquility, provide for the common defense, promote the general welfare, and secure the blessings of liberty to ourselves and our posterity, do ordain and establish this Constitution for the United States of America.

"The people" form the federal government, not the states.

"Common defense is the only specific reason mentioned. Others are intentionally vague.

ARTICLE I

1. Legislative powers; in whom vested

All legislative powers herein granted shall be vested in a Congress of the United States, which shall consist of a Senate and House of Representatives.

The Senate allows all states to have equal representation in the legislative branch

The House of Representatives is apportioned by population, giving more power directly to the people.

2. House of Representatives, how and by whom chosen
Qualifications of a Representative. Representatives and direct taxes, how apportioned. Enumeration. Vacancies to be filled. Power of choosing officers, and of impeachment.

The House of Representatives shall be composed of members chosen every second year by the people of the several States, and the elector in each State shall have the qualifications requisite for electors of the most numerous branch of the State Legislature. 2. No person shall be a Representative who shall not have attained the age of twenty-five years, and been seven years a citizen of the United States, and who shall not, when elected, be an inhabitant of that State in which he shall be chosen.
3. Representatives [and direct taxes] shall be apportioned among the several States which may be included within this Union, according to their respective numbers, [which shall be determined by adding the whole number of free persons, including those bound to service for a term of years, and excluding Indians not taxed, three-fifths of all other persons.] The actual enumeration shall be made within three years after the first meeting of the Congress of the United States, and within every subsequent term of ten years, in such manner as they shall by law direct. The number of Representatives shall not exceed one for every thirty thousand, but each State shall have at least one Representative; and until such enumeration shall be made, the State of New Hampshire shall be entitled to choose three, Massachusetts eight, Rhode Island and Providence Plantations one, Connecticut five, New York six, New Jersey four, Pennsylvania eight, Delaware one, Maryland six, Virginia ten, North Carolina five, South Carolina five, and Georgia three.

<<Altered by 14th Amendment>>

Representatives shall be apportioned among the several States according to their respective numbers, counting the whole number of persons in each State, excluding Indians not taxed. Representatives shall be apportioned among the several States according to their respective numbers, counting the whole number of persons in each State, excluding Indians not taxed. But when the right to vote at any election for the choice of Electors for President and Vice-President of the United States,

Representatives in Congress, the executive and judicial officers of a State, or the members of the Legislature thereof, is denied to any of the male inhabitants of such State, being twenty-one years of age, and citizens of the United States, or in any way abridged, except for participation in rebellion, or other crime, the basis of representation therein shall be reduced in the proportion which the number of such male citizens shall bear to the whole number of male citizens twenty-one years of age in such State.

Figure 3.2 Here is part of the U.S. Constitution in the center, with related commentary surrounding it. This is the same technique that is used with the Talmud (Fig. 3.1).

is just not enough space on any page to hold the vast amount of material that would have to fit close to the central text. Instead, imagine if the commentary were invisible but could be called up at the click of a mouse when the cursor is pointed at the relevant section. Now we have moved from nonlinearity to interactivity. Both the Talmud and the U.S. Constitution would benefit from such an interactive treatment. In particular, modern interactive access to the material provides a layout solution by allowing text to be hidden until it is needed. This same solution works well for situations in which a diagram needs to be annotated by what printers and graphic designers refer to as callouts. For example, Figure 3.3 shows an exploded drawing of a lightbulb using callouts.

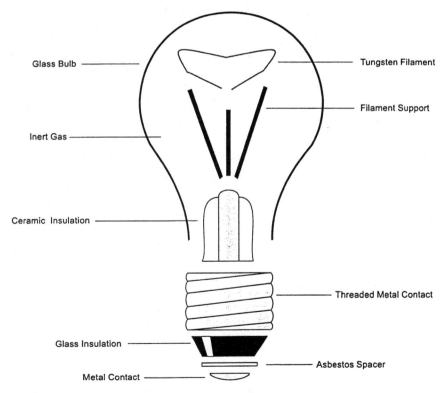

Figure 3.3 This diagram of a lightbulb shows what printers refer to as "callouts." If the drawing were very complex, these callouts could get very difficult to read as they overlap. Interactive media can hide these callouts until the user requests them by pointing to the objects. When interactive media do this, the results are called "rollovers."

This is useful because the visual layout is so efficient. If this were in an ebook, you could click on the parts of the drawing to reveal each callout interactively.

Maps provide another example of a problem in need of an interactive solution. In fact, maps form an entire subcategory of interactive publishing. There isn't enough space on most maps to print all the geographical features, cities, and towns without overprinting the text to the point of illegibility. This problem is only partially solved by having separate geographical, physical, and political maps. Imagine if you could plot one map and choose only what you wanted at any one time. A map of South America could simultaneously be a topographic map, a political map, and a road map, but each overlay is independent, and content is selectable. You could show all the cities and towns of a certain size so that the smaller or larger ones don't clutter the map. Of course, you could use a search engine to locate any place name on the map, saving a tremendous amount of time. Using interactivity, one map can be invisibly overlaid with different cartographic information.

The Rosetta Stone is a particularly interesting bit of archaeology, not for its content but for its presentation of content. The Rosetta Stone, shown in Figure 3.4, is a slab of black basalt that was discovered by Napoleon's troops in 1799. On it is inscribed a decree praising King Ptolemy V. The decree is written three times in three different languages: hieroglyphic, demotic, and Greek. Because Greek was known and the other languages were not, British physicist Thomas Young and French Egyptologist Jean Francoise Champollion were able to decipher the hieroglyphic and demotic languages by comparing them to the Greek. It is clear that the author or authors of the Rosetta Stone wanted its content to be understood by people who read different languages. Today, using interactive technology, we can choose the language we want to read or hear. In the same way that one interactive map can be overlaid with various kinds of cartographic information, interactive texts can be presented in many languages.

Because content determines whether interactivity will add anything useful to a subject, we have deliberately used examples from the pre-computer era. But today publishers and producers of traditional media often find themselves facing organizational, layout, structural, and design problems that could be solved using interactive technologies.

Figure 3.4 The Rosetta Stone is perhaps one of the earliest uses of interactive writing (although that is not likely to have been an intended use). The authors wrote the same text three times so that readers of Greek, Egyptian hieroglyphic, and demotic scripts could understand the decree praising King Ptolemy V. A result is that readers in any of these languages can translate the other two languages, and so they can decrypt two languages if they know only one. (Photo © Andrew Bonime).

Examples of Media that Can Benefit from Interactivity

Let's consider some examples of traditional media that benefit from the use of interactive computer technology; in fact, several of these already exist in interactive form. Also, this list is by no means exhaustive, but it is intended to illustrate some of the many ways in which interactive technology can help solve problems inherent in traditional media.

Interactive Nonfiction

Telephone and Other Directories.   This category includes all types of directories, including telephone books, college yearbooks, and industry directories such as the *Literary Market Place (LMP),* which contains information about book publishers. On one hand, directories may be of little interest to writers. Who, after all, has the *Los Angeles Yellow Pages* on their list of writing credits? More importantly, has anyone ever received royalties for this important work? Nevertheless, directories offer a good jumping off point to show how interactivity can solve content problems.

Electronic phone directories allow you to look up a name and get the phone number and street address more quickly than if you had to page through the print version. Moreover, you can look up a phone number and find the associated name and street address, or you can look up the street address and find every person who lives there (useful if you wanted to identify everyone in an apartment building). You can even get a listing of contiguous addresses, so you could find the phone numbers of all of your neighbors. Some people think this is scary, but you can only find what is listed; an unlisted number can't be found.

One other thing: An extraordinarily large amount of information takes up very little space in digital form, so it is possible to put every phone directory in the United States on about six standard CD-ROMs or one DVD-ROM. This data density can be very useful not only for the space saved but for the ability to cross-relate information that previously would have spanned several volumes.

When they are digitized, many directories shrink in absolute terms because redundancy is reduced. Consider, for example, the *Physicians' Desk Reference (PDR)*. This famous blue-bound book is several times longer than it needs to be because it lists the same information in four separate locations. A doctor can look up a drug by its generic name, its chemical name, its manufacturer, or its trade name. The interactive version of the PDR needs only one set of data because searching for a drug using any of those categories will get the user to the same entry. Therefore, you can look up the name of a manufacturer and the generic, trade, or chemical name for any drug and it produces the entire correct record for that drug. Clearly, directories rank among the most successful categories of new media because of their intrinsic need for interactivity.

College Catalogues.   College catalogues are essentially a type of directory and users benefit from the ability to search them electronically. In particular, the ability to search for combinations of data can make a catalogue more useful. For example, if you wanted to find all of the courses taught by a particular professor, the printed version of a college catalogue may not be useful, but if you used interactive technology it would be a snap. Similarly, you could find out all the courses required for your major, as well as the prerequisites. Using more complex programming, you could map out an entire academic year by choosing a major and a minor, listing all the necessary classes such that the prerequisites are scheduled in proper order, and developing an entire schedule for the degree program.

Manuals, Tutorials, and Training.   Any procedural manual can benefit as much from multimedia as from the organizational ability of interactive technology. While a manual can make the same use of searching and cus-tomizable organization as directories, manuals tend to deal with procedural descriptions that are best illustrated in video, animation, or a series of images with a voice-over narration. In a first-aid course, for example, it is nearly impossible to adequately explain the correct procedure for perform-ing CPR using only text and pictures in a book. Imagine how effective a narrated animated sequence could be. You might say: "Why not just do it all on videotape?" The answer is that videotape is linear and does not allow the use of any useful interactive tools, such as searching or information organization, which facilitate access and hence increase the content's value.

Tutorials allow the user to follow along and actually perform some of the tasks being taught. Any task that can be represented on a screen with user input via a mouse, touch screen, or some other device can be very helpful in learning situations because the user gets instant feedback. Consider, for example, a training manual for an automotive course: A wiring diagram could be shown on the screen along with a text-based or voice-over diagnosis indicating that the car's horn is broken. The student could actually draw the correct wiring on the screen, testing different pos-sible solutions until the horn functions properly (signaled by a honk from the speakers). This can be accompanied by many different interactive tech-niques that guide the student, keep test score results, and track improve-ment in the student's abilities.

Computer-Based Training (CBT) and Computer-Aided Instruction (CAI). Computer-based training and computer-aided instruction have been around as interactive teaching tools for a long time, teaching, for example, foreign languages. In the past, they were often implemented by complex hookups of laser disc players and computers. Now, CBT and CAI are done largely by compact self-contained systems, such as computers with CD-ROM drives, or by online systems. The potential improvements are enormous.

Maps.   We have already seen how maps benefit from an interactive technology's ability to hide extra information displaying only what is needed at any one time. When maps are digitized, they take up far less space than they do in print. When combined with a basic search capability, this makes maps a prime beneficiary of interactive technology. It is possible to put a searchable street map of the entire United States on a single disc, and use it as the basis for a car navigation system.

Travel Guides.   Travel guides can make use of many of the tools that interactive technology has to offer: the ability to search and locate any town, city, sightseeing point of interest, and so on, can be combined with the previously discussed capability of interactive maps and multimedia. This is a category that continues to make use of advanced technology as it develops. The *Global Positioning System (GPS)* allows a device to locate your position accurately anywhere in the world. These devices can be as small as a wristwatch, and they can display the position of the user on a screen showing a map stored on disc, in solid state memory, or in another storage medium. By combining this technology with interactive and multimedia technologies, it is possible to display your location on a street map. Moreover, a travel guide can tell you to "Turn left at the next street, then make a right at the fountain. The Ponte Vecchio is on your left." Or it could say, "Don't go any further up this street or you will end up in an unsafe neighborhood."

One advantage that interactive technologies have over books is size. It is easy to get bogged down with guidebooks and literature on a trip. When you go to Europe, for example, it would be beneficial to take only those portions of the guidebooks that pertain to the countries or cities you plan to visit. You could take a miniature computer (in the form of a handheld information device), or you could use CD-ROM or online services on your home computer and print out the relevant sections. Both of these methods take advantage of an interactive technology's capability to search and organize relevant information.

Language Translators.   Language translators (as opposed to language training systems, addressed earlier in "Manuals, Tutorials, and Training") make use of the computer's ability to search for and locate information. In essence, when you enter a phrase in one language, the system searches the database of the other language to find a match. Of course, language is not very exact and its success depends on correctly determining context and nuance in addition to following rules that differ from language to language. For these reasons, language translation technology is far from exact, and often useless if it is expected to replace a flesh-and-blood translator. However, it is useful for phrases and individual words such as numbers and days of the week. Interactive technologies can also enhance language translation by offering audio pronunciations.

Compendia.   Any book that combines categories of facts or small chunks of information (such as books of quotations) can make use of the organizational capabilities of interactive ebook media. Examples of these include almanacs, restaurant and hotel guides, books of various lists (such as "best of . . ." lists) and fact books. By using the search capability of interactive technology, the user can create customized lists of subjects, facts, or categories. For example, you could find all the breeds of dog that would be a good pet in a small apartment and that get along well with children. Then you could read about each of the breeds on this newly created list without having to search for each of them.

Books about Other Media.   Imagine trying to write the biography of Beethoven without being able to offer your readers his music. This type of problem has been addressed using traditional media by bundling an audiocassette or compact disc with the paper book. But that doesn't integrate the audio with the text in a very useful way. To be truly valuable, the author needs to be able to discuss the music and then (metaphorically) to say, "Listen to this." The ability to play audio and video in context is something that interactive technologies do very well. The ebook user can experience cogent examples of what is referenced in the text and replay them at will.

If you are authoring a work about any of the media that exist outside of the static visual realm of text and still graphics, such as movies, television, music, or theater, interactive multimedia may be the best way to present it.

Dictionaries.   Dictionaries are such obvious beneficiaries of interactive technology that handheld electronic dictionaries from companies like Franklin already outsell the print versions. Interactive technology provides the capability to search for any word, which eliminates the "look up" chore. Moreover, some electronic dictionaries solve the age-old problem of how to check a word's spelling when you don't know how to spell it. Instead, the dictionary accepts your best guess and supplies possible correctly spelled words.

Ebook dictionaries also allow a type of function that paper dictionaries have always lacked: internal searching. For example, a user can search for the word *animal* and find not only its definition but also its occurrence throughout definitions of other words. This would lead the user to definitions of other animals, such as dog, cat, or *foramanifera.*

Aside from the search capability, interactive dictionaries can offer audio pronunciations, as well as video and animated examples.

Encyclopedias.   Encyclopedias and encyclopedic reference works benefit from the application of interactive technologies in the same way as dictionaries, but they also benefit from the application of multimedia that can help illustrate and explain techniques and processes that are difficult to describe otherwise. If a picture is worth a thousand words, then animation or video, as well as audio, may well be worth a thousand pictures.

How-To Books.   Any book or video that describes how to build a house, tend a garden, train a dog, repair a car, climb a mountain, or even use a computer, can benefit from interactive technologies. For example, let's consider a videotape entitled *How to Build Your Own House,* based on a printed book of the same name. As with the paper book, the videotape is organized according to the tasks involved in home building, including selecting the site, pouring the foundation, framing the house, installing the electric and telephone wiring, putting in the plumbing and heating, and so on. The book version cannot show the activities in full action—only still photographs; but it does allow nonsequential access—you can turn directly to the section on plumbing without going through the section on pouring the foundation.

The video version shows the actual processes in ways that the book cannot. You can see the concrete foundation actually being poured and the electrical wiring being inserted into the walls. Although you can access the contents nonsequentially, it isn't easy. If you want to get to the section on plumbing, you need to fast forward and guess where to stop. Many "how-to" videotapes provide some sort of counter system for locating the various parts, but they are unwieldy and not especially accurate. Besides, they waste time while the tape is fast forwarding or reversing.

Clearly, interactive ebook technologies can improve both the paper book and its videotaped version of the book. An interactive ebook may feature a table of contents on the first screen. The user can click on the word or icon for wiring and instantly watch the video on installing electrical outlets—without having to fast forward or reverse. Of course, all of the benefits of any interactive title apply here as well, including the ability to search throughout, print out sections (plans, diagrams, and so on), and hear audio narration when necessary.

Health Information and Diagnosis.   Books dealing with health and medicine have inherent problems with information organization. In fact, the problem with the majority of these books is that the information may be there but locating just what you want can be daunting. In some cases, the technical vocabulary can be a serious barrier. Search and retrieval functions and the user's ability to create customized organizational structure can be of immense help in turning data into useable information. Interactive technologies make it possible to locate diseases by symptom, physiological function, or bodily system. In fact, diagnosis becomes possible in a way that is impossible in a paper book.

Let's say that you are a medical writer and you want the reader to be able to diagnose a medical problem by answering yes or no to a series of branching questions. Figure 3.5 shows a flowchart with questions and a branching structure leading to a diagnosis or a course of action. In fact, several medical books contain diagrams such as these. But a far more effective way to accomplish the same result, as shown in Figure 3.6, is to have the questions appear on the screen either in text, audio, and/or video format and allow the user to select a Yes or No button that automatically jumps to the next question. In this system the flowchart is internalized, so instead of seeing all of the questions in the entire branching structure, the user has to deal only with questions relevant to the particular path taken.

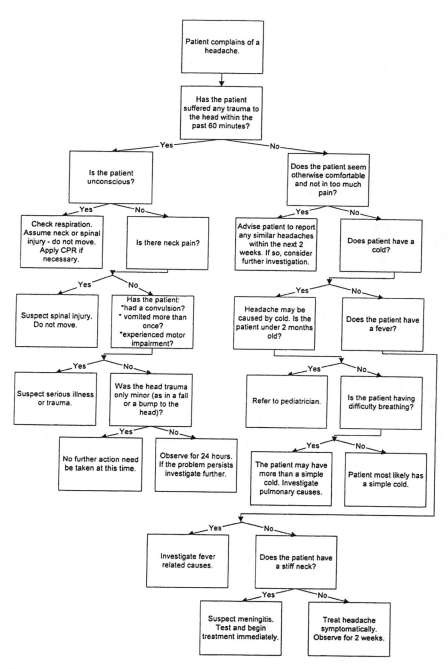

Figure 3.5 A flowchart for a medical diagnostic title using "Yes/No" answers to arrive at a diagnosis.

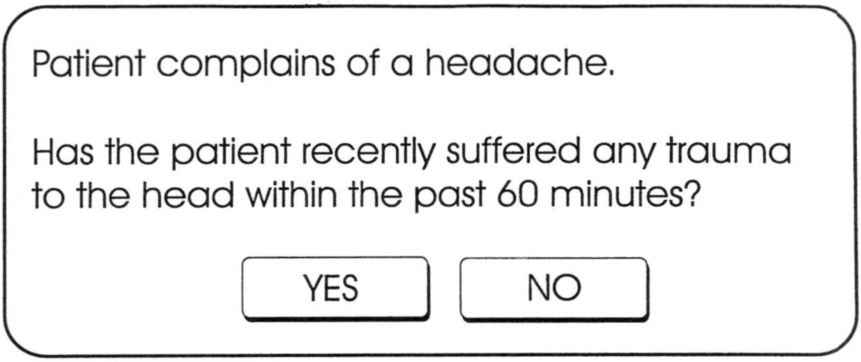

Patient complains of a headache.

Has the patient recently suffered any trauma to the head within the past 60 minutes?

YES   NO

Figure 3.6 A question with a Yes and a No button. By using a series of questions with yes/no answers, the entire branching structure is hidden. The user can therefore navigate a complex set of questions, which then can produce useful answers to compound questions.

In addition, multimedia can provide animated examples of first-aid techniques such as the Heimlich maneuver or CPR, integrated into the appropriate portions of the information structure.

Interactive Journalism.   Until the explosion in popularity of the World Wide Web (the Web), interactive journalism was impractical. In the time it takes to produce, replicate, and distribute CD-ROMs, the news would no longer be current. The Web changed all that. The Web can have as much immediacy as a news broadcast and more immediacy than a newspaper. By adding multimedia, the content can juxtapose an audio or video recording of a political speech with a printed commentary. Stories can be linked so that rich background information is always available as the user reads the current news story. Likewise, editorials and news analyses can be linked to news stories and to each other. Also, background information can be linked directly to current content. An article about defense could link the acronym NATO not only to its expanded title North Atlantic Treaty Organization, but to other articles about its history and organization.

Interactive journalism uniquely combines features from broadcast journalism and print journalism with new computer-based capabilities of hyperlinking and searching. This category of interactive media is vast in its potential.

Interactive Fiction

To this point, we have mainly discussed nonfiction writing, but new interactive technologies have also created opportunities for fiction writers. The adaptation of new technology to fiction writing, however, is not nearly as obvious. In fact, one could argue that traditional fiction does not truly benefit from interactivity.

Fiction, by its very nature, is the product of the creative mind of the writer and perhaps does not require the search or information organization capabilities offered by interactive media. Instead, it could be argued that the point of writing fiction is exactly to impose the writer's organizational flow on the reader and not to allow deviation from it.

However, as with any art form, fiction writing undoubtedly will evolve in response to interactive technology. New technologies offer creative opportunities, and experimental fiction writers are actively inventing new kinds of interactive prose. For example, some authors create their fiction novels "live" on Web pages, and many fiction newsgroups allow group participation in the writing process. It remains to be seen whether interactive fiction will endure as have print, filmed, and performed fiction.

User-Selectable Multiple-Plot Branching and Character and Environmental Attributes.   One type of interactive fiction allows the user to select different plot paths. The writer creates a story shell that includes the characters and a general theme of environment and events. At several points in the narrative, the user is presented with choices that determine the direction of the immediate and/or the overall plot. This consists of many different path combinations and many different beginnings, middles, and endings. It is also possible to add the dimension of character and environmental attributes to the story branching so that the user may choose the psychological makeup of the main or subordinate characters in the story. This could also have an impact on the plot, and the plot choices may affect aspects of the characters' personalities. In fact, the dynamic impact of the user setting in motion different character attributes can become so convoluted that the result is a simulation of reality with predetermined (but user-selectable) attributes.

There is an entire category of simulation software available (usually with the prefix *sim* in the title, as in *Sim City*) that allows users to create total environments ranging from ant farms to human civilizations and observe how their selections impact the environment's development. This category of software has been called, not surprisingly, *Artificial Life*.

As we shall see in Chapter 17, the writer must be extremely careful to maintain control of the original creative idea because the possibilities for mutation are very seductive. If you do not adhere to some very important rules, an interactive story can end up as nothing more than an interesting game. Of course, that may be just what the writer had in mind.

Hand-Eye Games.   Without a doubt, games have been the most successful of all interactive media categories, and the most successful games (with certain exceptions) tend to be what game designers call "twitch" games. These are fast-moving arcade-style games that rely on expert hand-eye coordination—an arguably important educational skill, at least for the future generation of jet fighter pilots.

It may seem odd to cite games in a book targeted at writers, but these games are created by writers. In general, there is an implied back story or exposition in a game that sets the scene for the action at the core. For example, a game might be based on the notion that an outer space chemical facility has been taken over by alien creatures of varying degrees of physical prowess. The user is the only one who can save the facility and is armed with an array of weapons, some of which can destroy these alien creatures, others that only weaken them. Most hand-eye game plots boil down to "kill or be killed," but with sufficient creative force and higher technological investment, they could develop into a form of genuine fiction. For example, the ability to create artificial realities that are freely navigable by users could open the floodgates for creative fiction.

Environmental Exploration.   Another type of game that has been enormously successful is the environmental exploration game as exemplified by a title called *Myst*. The principle behind this type of game is deceptively simple: The writer creates an environment with a geographical setting such as a remote island or isolated (read "haunted") house or castle. A background story is created to accompany this environment, which in itself can consist of a rich plot and characters. The user finds him or herself in this environment and has to accomplish some goal. This goal can be to escape, to rescue someone, to discover some sort of buried treasure, or a combination of these objectives. The point is that the user is immersed in a story that has already taken place. In this way, the writer needn't deal with interactions with existing characters and events. The user can only react to what has already occurred.

Summary

To be effective, interactivity should solve some sort of problem inherent in the content. Even before the advent of interactive technology, books had to deal with these problems that today can be solved by the application of interactive media. There are many types of content that can benefit from the application of interactive technology in both nonfiction and fiction writing. Whereas applications of interactive technology to nonfiction writing are often direct, applications to fiction writing are more subtle and necessarily subject to creative whim.

Linear Writing Versus Interactive Writing

But I digress. . . .

—Anonymous

Hypertext and Hypermedia: A Web, Not a Chain

At the core of modern interactivity is hypertext and its multimedia twin, hypermedia. The word *hypertext* was coined in 1965 by Theodore Nelson to describe the use of computers to express the nonlinear structure of written ideas. This type of nonlinearity stands in contrast to the linear format of books, film, and speech. In hypertext, words are linked to other words that exist in other parts of a work or in other works altogether. Words that have these links are called *hot words, hot links, hyperlinks,* or just *links.*

Before the computer was introduced as a medium of expression, it was very difficult, if not impossible, to express ideas the way they are formed in our minds. Human thought consists of a linked network of individual ideas, recollections, and images, many of which may be seemingly unrelated in content but have some relationship to the others nonetheless. In contrast, books present ideas as a series of links moving sequentially from one to the next. The sequence is predetermined by the author. The same is true of films and even speech.

Hypertext lets us present ideas in a manner that closely resembles the way in which we think. In addition, it allows ideas to be linked into a larger, more contextual whole. Hypertext allows the author to express ideas without having to adhere to the often constricting need to place them in a specific order. Hypertext likewise frees the user to investigate an idea or a series of ideas according to a personal way of thinking and to familiarity with the background information. Hypertext makes learning more enjoyable, and enhances data retention because hypertext is more efficient at meshing the information with the user's thought process than a linear presentation of ideas can be.

In the linear format of a book or film, the user reads or hears the information in a specific order. As one idea sparks curiosity for others, the information arrives at the user's brain in strict adherence to a predetermined order that may or may not coincide with the user's particular interest at that time. Because of this, the user may be thinking about something other than the next idea in the linear chain of ideas. With hyperlinking, the user can read, listen to, or watch the presentation of an idea and investigate a path according to the many possible branches in the web of ideas. This process is effective because the information arrives at the user's brain in direct response to the user's curiosity. In this way, information can be presented by an author so that each user individualizes it to suit a personal thought process.

Although hypertext was originally limited to the text-based expression of ideas, the subsequent introduction of multimedia allowed text, images, audio, and video to be interlinked as well. Thus, ideas that cannot be expressed in text can be linked together with those that can. This even more closely follows the pattern of human thought because much thought is not limited to verbal expression. The addition of multimedia has expanded the notion of hypertext to hypermedia.

By presenting ideas in a nonlinear structure, these ideas are presented unprejudiced by group assignment or the order in which they are presented. This leads to more freedom on the part of the user, and allows the user to create pathways of investigation. Hypertext and hypermedia have the following characteristics:

- They present ideas nonsequentially.
- They follow the thought process.
- They allow users to choose individual pathways through the information.
- They allow information to transcend individual documents.
- They link text with pictures, audio, and video.

Hypertext and Hypermedia in Action

The way hypertext is employed is quite simple: The author marks the words to be linked and specifies the target of the link. The process of inserting hyperlinks is similar to inserting footnotes, endnotes, or bibliographies, except that with hyperlinks you can have the equivalent of a footnote inside a footnote. Instead of simply referring the user to another work or document, the author can insert links to documents that themselves contain links to other documents. Sometimes the links can connect similar types of documents, such as a collection of Shakespeare's plays. These cross-references may themselves contain links to yet other works, forming a rich web of interlinked information.

Alternatively, the ability to search several documents might produce the effect of hyperlinking. If the user performs a search and the particular document is listed in the search findings, then the document is de facto linked to the other documents listed in the same search through the document list itself, which contains links to all the documents.

The World Wide Brain

As we have seen, it is possible to use hypertext to link a single document internally with multiple pathways within its own data structure. Moreover, because today's computers can be linked easily with one another via international communication lines, it is possible to link up documents residing in computers all over the world. The user investigating a pathway in one document may find that the path leads to another document halfway around the world. That document in turn may link to others residing in different computers, and so on. Because the links follow seamlessly (there is no announcement saying: "You have left the Encyclopedia Britannica and are now entering the National Library in The Hague"), the user has the experience of reading a single worldwide web of information. The network of computers linked by the common use of special hypertext/hypermedia software is called the *World Wide Web*. We'll discuss the Web in more detail in Chapter 22, but you can skip ahead if you want.

Difficulties of Hypertext Writing

Writers accustomed to linear writing may find it difficult to embrace a nonlinear structure because they have learned to present ideas hierarchically. Writers are trained to develop ideas so that the reader learns the fundamentals first, and then each successive idea builds from the previous one. In nonlinear writing, readers can choose any pathway into and within the structure. This means that they might read about something without first being exposed to any foundation provided by the writer. To anticipate this, writers must learn to present ideas so that they are self-contained. Readers who desire more background can then find the information they need to expand the scope of the foreground material.

Of course, interactive writing covers many different types of structure, just as any type of writing does. So it is important to understand that some types of structure are easier than others to adapt to interactive treatment. For example, a dictionary has an inherently nonhierarchical structure. Readers do not build their knowledge base from a foundation. Dictionary information consists of short, self-contained citations in the form of definitions. Entries can be easily hyperlinked with cross-references. (In the preinteractive era this was handled by printing *see . . .*).

In other works, such as a biography, interactive writers may feel distinctly uncomfortable discussing inherently chronological events out of sequence. They may feel that it is necessary to set up exposition and then build information based on previously presented information. They may find it difficult to write a narrative with small chunks of self-contained information. In fact, the difficulty is very real. As a result, good interactive nonfiction writing requires a level of inventiveness more often found in creative works.

In the 1941 film *Citizen Kane*, screenwriters Orson Welles and Herman Mankiewicz wrote a linear biographical story in a nonlinear fashion. Instead of presenting the events in the life of the protagonist Charles Foster Kane in sequential order, they were shown as recollections of people who had known Kane. Using secondary characters to tell the story of Kane's life, the screenwriters had to solve the problems of overlap in the chronology and the artificial breaks in the seemingly natural flow of biographical narrative. The resulting screenplay demonstrates that even an inherently chronological story can be effectively expressed in a nonlinear manner, provided the writer is sufficiently creative.

However, it is important to note in this example that the screenwriters controlled the structure of the narrative. Even though the story was presented in an unorthodox manner, the writers determined the order of the scenes and their content throughout. If *Citizen Kane* were interactive, the viewer would have been able to choose any character's point of view at any time. Clearly, this would have compounded the challenge of writing the work.

Examples of Interactivity

To help illustrate the concepts of interactive writing, three examples are provided below. In each case, we'll discuss possibilities for interactivity along with some limitations. Adding interactive elements to each of these examples should help you to begin thinking in terms of interactive content and structure.

An Example of Interactive Narrative: The Setag Family

Let's take a look at a simple narrative form and see how it could be expressed using interactive media.

The Setags are a typical dysfunctional family. Mr. Setag is head of a high-tech company in Silicon Valley. The pressures of running the company have taken a toll on his relationship with Mrs. Setag. In fact, the problems are so great that they have discussed getting a divorce. However, they are trying to stay together for the sake of their son, Billy.

In a linear novel, the author probably would pick a character and tell the story from that point of view. Of course, the author could change points of view and that would add a level of interest for the reader. Many novelists use this technique to good effect. We could view the Setags from the point of view of Mr. Setag, Mrs. Setag, Billy, or even the family dog, Woof. If it's true that every situation has several truths, the readers would benefit from seeing these different perspectives. This could be done in noninteractive media, but the presentation would not allow the reader to make the decisions or to switch points of view at will.

By using interactive media, readers could follow the story through the eyes of any character from beginning to end. Readers could also view individual events through the eyes of all characters. Interactive readers are empowered through the choices offered by interactivity. By combining the users' ability to select point of view with their ability to select a narrative pathway, a rich creative process begins to evolve. Figure 4.1 shows a simple flow diagram for part of this interactive fiction story.

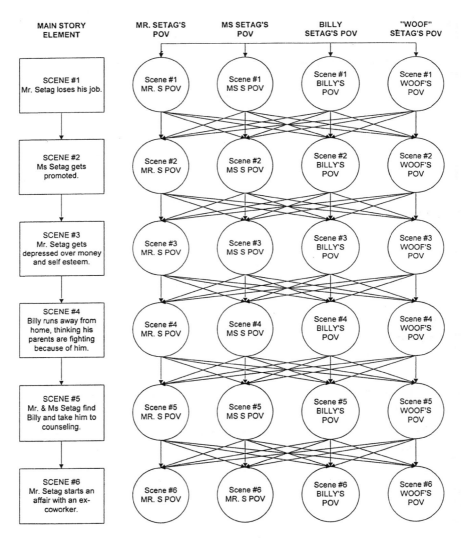

Figure 4.1 A linear story progression with changeable point of view (POV). The top line, with its down-pointing arrows, shows that the user can shift POV while remaining on the same story level. Doing this does not advance the story but shows the same event through a different character's vantage point. The diagonal lines show the progression of the story through different characters' POV. If the story were nonlinear the possibilities would be geometrically more complex, because each character's POV at each stage of the story could link not only to another character's POV at the same or another level of the story, but it could link as well from any character to any other character and any event in the story.

On the other hand, interactive fiction can end up like a restaurant where patrons are invited to cook the meal for themselves—it can be a novel experience, but there is no skilled creator in charge. Many fiction devotees will prefer that the writer not just provide the ingredients, but blend and cook them as well.

Interactive fiction must, by definition, allow the user to have full control over the plot and any other elements the writer chooses to provide (such as character traits). The writer will not be able to develop the plot and character in a particularly well-crafted manner because all of the pieces must be made to fit in a multitude of ways in order to provide the user with enough flexibility to enjoy the process over time. To use yet another analogy: This process is more like a paint-by-numbers project than the work of a true artist.

An Example of Interactive Reference: A Travel Guide to the Caribbean

If you're one of those less adventurous people who won't travel to the other side of your hometown without a travel guide, then you'll appreciate the possibilities of interactivity for travel writers. If you were planning a trip to the Caribbean, you might just check the airfare and book the cheapest flight. But if you've ever visited Puerto Rico during hurricane season, you'll probably want to try a more thorough approach.

In a linear version of a Caribbean travel guide, the writer simply lists each island and describes the culture, opportunities for sightseeing, accommodations, and restaurants. Charts may be added to summarize the various attractions. But for the person planning a vacation, it would also be useful to be able to list the most desirable features and to search for those islands that meet the criteria. With interactive media, the user could say, "I want to go to the Caribbean in the fall; I want to go where they have the best scuba diving and gambling; I want gourmet food, but I don't want to dress up for dinner; I'm not interested in golf or tennis; and I only have five days and two thousand dollars to spend."

Of course, the user will also want in-depth information about each island. For this reason, an alphabetical index should be provided as well. A map of the Caribbean should also be provided, as should maps of each island. Using multimedia, it would be possible, for example, to show aerial

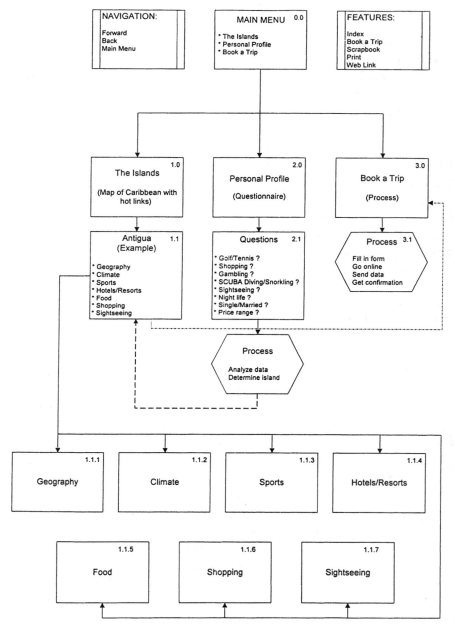

Figure 4.2 This flow diagram for an interactive program on the Caribbean shows a typical layout for an informational title.

The box to the left of the Main Menu lists the navigational features that will appear on every screen. The Forward and Back choices can appear as arrows or as words. When inappropri-

footage of each island so the user could see the layout of coastlines and mountains. (In Chapter 23 we'll consider how much audio and video can fit on a disc, and the effect of bandwidth on multimedia delivery online). Figure 4.2 shows part of an interactive flow diagram for a Caribbean travel guide.

---

ate, they will be grayed out. (For example, to a user on the Main Menu, the Main Menu navigational choice would make no sense, so there it would be unavailable.)

The box to the right of the Main Menu lists the features that will appear on every page. The Index will list all topics on the disc, such as names of islands, cities, and towns; hotels; geographic features; shopping locations; and so on. Users wishing to find something they already know about may choose this feature, which will produce an alphabetical list of these items. Each item on the list is hyperlinked to its topic area, so clicking on any item links directly to its context.

The Book a Trip feature is context sensitive. The user can go to it to book a trip from any screen. Book a Trip can also be reached via the Main Menu; the user can fill in a form and then set the process in motion.

The Scrapbook is a cumulative copy-and-paste center that allows users to "collect" data as they explore the title. Later they can print out this information or copy it into a word processing program.

Print allows the user to print out any screen full of information. That could include text, maps, or images.

Web Link allows the user to go online, access the World Wide Web, and log onto the site that is determined by the programming of the title. If, for example, the disc had been produced by a travel magazine, Web Link could go directly to the magazine's home page. Alternatively, the link could be context sensitive, in which case it might go to a page associated with the island that is currently on screen.

Each Main Menu item is numbered using a decimal system. This numbering system is extremely helpful in the development of titles with large number of multimedia assets. In this way assets can be numbered according to the screens with which they are associated. Usually storyboards that correspond with each screen in the title will be generated. These storyboards contain all the text and multimedia elements along with layout information. The numbering system on the flowchart corresponds with the numbering system used with the storyboard.

In this example, we show only one third-level result (Antigua). Assuming the second level (1.0) is a map of the Caribbean, the user can click on any island, producing the next level—the island's main screen. If we assume Antigua is 1.1, the other islands would be numbered 1.2, 1.3, 1.4, and so on. The next level takes its number from the island and adds another decimal point. Thus the next level, which shows features of each island, would refer to the island and the feature screen. So the Geography screen for Antigua is 1.1.1 as shown, and the Geography screen for Bonaire might be 1.2.1.

There are two processes shown. One, the Personal Profile, allows users to answer questions about their travel preferences. Using a database associated with the title, the program determines the best island that suits each user's criteria. Instead of simply displaying an island's name, the program calls up the island's profile screen. Then the user can explore the island or book a trip using the Book a Trip feature.

Using a nonlinear approach, travel writers can provide a great deal of information without worrying about its effect on the narrative. Users can locate exactly what they need and still retain the ability to browse through the material.

An Example of Interactive Reference: History of the French Revolution

We all know that history happens in sequential order. We know this because we struggled to remember important dates in history class. But in writing about historic events and periods, it is often very difficult to convey important ideas in strictly linear form. For example, the French Revolution is difficult to describe because it cannot be sufficiently explained as a series of events. The French Revolution is rich with personalities, social issues, economic issues, and events that often require a simultaneous view. For the history to make sense, a writer describing events in France in 1789 might find it necessary to deviate from the linear narrative quite often to provide background on key figures and social movements. Some readers may be familiar with some of these events while others might not be. The linear writer must therefore make assumptions about the reader's familiarity with some of these facts at the outset and maintain that level throughout.

In contrast, using interactive media events could be laid out in linear form, with background information linked to each historical figure, social movement, and so on. Thus, instead of having to pause in the narrative to provide background information on Robespierre, for example, the writer could simply link the name Robespierre in the narrative to a biographical section and give all the pertinent information in detail there. Readers unfamiliar with Robespierre could take the side trip to learn about him, then resume the narrative. Of course, the side trip doesn't have to end there. A biography of Robespierre could contain hyperlinks with background information about other historic events, social and economic movements, and so on.

Summary

Hypertext and hypermedia describe the ability of computers to present ideas nonsequentially. This nonsequential structure more closely resembles the way ideas are formed in our minds and is more versatile than the linear form used by print, movies, and speech. Hyperlinking connects ideas in the form of a web rather than a chain. Writers sometimes have difficulty writing in a nonlinear structure because they are accustomed to writing hierarchically. In interactive writing, useful information can be provided for readers at any level of familiarity with the subject matter by linking the narrative to background information.

5

The Role of the Writer
in Interactive Media

Right now it's only a notion, but I think I can get money to make it into a concept
. . . and later turn it into an idea.

—Woody Allen (from Annie Hall)

Interactive technologies create writing opportunities that span a broad spectrum of styles, formats, and disciplines. As we have seen, possibilities range from fiction to nonfiction, from reference to how-to. Clearly, the role of the writer in each of these formats varies tremendously. The SASE (self-addressed stamped envelope) may have given way to e-mail, but rest assured, the rejection letter is still very much with us.

As with traditional writing, some interactive work is for hire and some of it is self-generated. Because interactive technologies employ distribution models and cost structures that differ greatly from their print counterparts, the electronic writer's role can be either easier or more difficult depending on whether, for example, the work is to be distributed online or as part or all of a CD-ROM.

Generally, because writing for many of the new media greatly depends on their multimedia content, the production model is most akin to that of a motion picture or a television show. However, because of the sophistication of the authoring tools, the number of people actually employed to create an interactive title is usually far fewer. Of course, that variable ultimately depends on the talents of individual contributors.

The Team

Each multimedia project is unique. Some can be accomplished by one author who performs all of the jobs; others have large, movielike teams of artists, programmers, writers, animators, musicians, and so on. On an elaborate CD-ROM or interactive television project or online, the team structure can vary, but it generally consists of the following members.

Producer

The producer is in charge of the production team. This person is responsible for the overall look and design concept, and for developing and maintaining the schedule and budget. As with a movie project, the producer is the central coordinator for all job functions. In fact, this is the person to be nicest to—producers are the ones who hire the writers. However, with interactive media, the producer's job encompasses job functions that in a movie production would be in the director's domain because there is no director on most interactive projects. If sequences of film must be shot or voice-overs must be recorded, and if either involves actors, then there may be a separate producer for these sequences; otherwise, the project producer will fill this role. In these cases, the producer functions in much the same way as a film director.

The producer generally is responsible for the overall vision and interactive functionality. Producers also must be able to write detailed documents, variously called *design specifications, production specifications,* or *functional specifications.* These documents describe every aspect of an interactive title, detailing every screen and every mouse click. The production team will use these documents, along with the flowchart, to build the title. Most producers also write proposals. In the case of a corporate or business-to-business project, the producer is responsible for client contact, maintenance of budgets and schedules, and putting out the many brush fires that emerge from the problems attendant to any interactive project.

Producers may be passionately involved with the creative vision of a project or they might just be bean counters, responsible for keeping the project on schedule and on budget. Most are a little of both.

Where Do They Come From?   Producers of interactive media generally have a similar background to producers in film, television, music, or advertising. However, interactive producers can also emerge from other disciplines involved in the creation of an interactive title, including art direction, computer programming, or even, yes, writing. In any case, the ideal producer is a person who can stay cool under pressure, keep the entire team happy, and knows how to work with spreadsheets and scheduling software. The producer needs to have enough savvy with the technology to communicate with the programmers, enough design capability to communicate with designers and artists, and enough familiarity with the subject to communicate with the subject experts or writers on the project. Finally, producers need to be able to write very good proposals, because that is where most projects begin.

Design Director (or Creative Director)

The design director is responsible for the graphic look of an ebook or Web site. The design director, who thus has expertise in media design and training or experience in interactive layout, hires and supervises teams of graphic designers and artists and establishes the design standard for the project. Sometimes the design director will personally create the art. From the cinematic point of view, the design director is a combination of art director, set designer, and director of photography. Creative directors function as they do in advertising, supervising the creation and selection of all production assets, including animation and photography as well as the creation and selection of all artwork to be used in the title.

Where Do They Come From?   Design directors are often escapees from magazine and advertising art departments or from book or package design departments. In any case, they are experienced in the design and layout of print media. They usually have a college or art school design education. With the exception of television news graphics departments, they rarely come from movie or television design departments because the skills needed in interactive design require expertise in print layout orientation. This is because, at least for now, computer screen visuals generally follow the paradigm of the printed page.

Interactive Designer

Unlike the design director, the interactive designer is concerned with the interactive workings of the ebook or Web site. This includes the information hierarchy, branching, and access to features such as searching. This job involves training in and knowledge of the perceptual and psychological aspects of the project layout and design. While concerned with the graphics and overall look and feel of the interface and design, the interactive designer is more concerned with the way users will relate to and interact with the content so that it is accessible and intuitive and allows the smoothest path possible to the information.

Interactive designers generally spend many hours observing focus groups working with actual interactive content to see how real people work with the ebooks or online content they have helped to develop. They also often monitor responses from actual users of finished products to see how products can be better designed in the future. Good interactive designers will develop a sense of what works, with particular attention to navigation and interface design.

Unfortunately, with budgets under tight scrutiny, many projects do not have an interactive designer. In this case, the job is generally split among the producer, the writer, and the design director.

Where Do They Come From?   Interactive designers come from many disciplines, including graphic design, marketing, education, training, and testing. They may even come from the world of writing.

Software Engineer/Programmer

To normal people, a listing of computer programming code may read like a quantum physics text written in Sanskrit, but here's all you have to know: Software is the list of hidden instructions that the computer uses to do whatever it does. These instructions are written in code. Writing code is tedious work, requiring the kind of person who can spend long periods of time on detailed, logical information written in arcane code, eat a lot of pizza, not get out much, and output truly impressive work. Because of its complexity, programming is often done by teams, so that the work can be divided and delegated. In general, a software engineer is the individual at the head of this team. This person designs the overall flow of the programming, breaks it up into sections, and assigns each section to a programmer.

There are different types of programming on interactive projects. Some involve the most fundamental type, dealing with the creation of functionality for a computer program. These programmers generally work in computer languages such as C or C++ or Visual Basic. But there are some authoring programs, such as Macromedia's Director, which are used by a great many programmers to develop interactive multimedia titles and interactive multimedia for the Web. Director uses a programming language called Lingo, which provides special functions to the actions and interactions of a Director-based multimedia project. Lingo programmers may or may not be able to write code in other languages.

Where Do They Come From?   Software engineers generally have at least an undergraduate degree in computer science or electrical engineering, and many have graduate degrees as well, but many others are self-taught. However they acquire the skill set, programmers tend to be on the young side—in their early twenties. This is partially a function of the newness of the field and partially because young people tend to be more attuned to the programmer's lifestyle, which often involves long hours and little time for anything else. Programmers often move into managerial positions after a few years.

Media (Asset) Integrator

The job of putting the illustrations, photos, video and audio clips, and text together into one interactive program falls to the media or asset integrator. This person works with one of the interactive product development programs, such as Macromedia's Director or eMedia's mTropolis to put all of the media assets together into a functioning program. This job may involve a certain amount of programming if the design of the project calls for special functions (such as performing a search). Sometimes the media integrator does this programming, but in other cases the programming is done by a programmer or software engineer who knows the specific programming language needed.

Where Do They Come From?   Media integrators can be programmers, designers, or artists who developed a skill set that makes them ideal for this work. Many are self-taught; others have learned these skills from exposure to other media integrators while working on other aspects of interactive projects. They need good organizational skills and a personality suited to long hours of tedious work (although not as tedious as straight programming).

Media Technicians

Because all interactive media is digital, someone has to put the various media assets (audio, video, and still pictures) into digital form. Various technicians and engineers are needed to digitize the media, perform some editing and quality enhancements, and send the digital file to the media integrator or an asset librarian. Although these functions can be handled by novice technicians or skilled engineers, media technicians must be skilled in the use of computer-based digital hardware and software.

Where Do They Come From?   Media technicians may come from colleges and universities that teach audio or video engineering. Many come from similar jobs in allied fields: recording or broadcast studios or post-production facilities.

Information Architect or Data Designer

If a project is text-intensive, someone must determine how the data will be organized and how it will be accessed. An information architect (sometimes called a data designer), the person with this training and skill, usually is part of the team during the early design phase. The information architect will determine many of the issues that affect the writer most closely: which types of data will be the main text and which will be the sidebar or subordinate modifying text. This person may be trained in information science or just may have a good sense of organization and information systems structure.

Where Do They Come From?   Information architects may have worked in publishing or information systems. In earlier lives they may have been editors or writers. They may also come from library science or information management jobs in an academic or corporate environment.

Webmaster

As you might have guessed, the Webmaster is responsible for creating, designing, programming, and maintaining a Web site on the World

Wide Web. This job differs from the other jobs we've mentioned because the job of a Webmaster generally doesn't end when a specific project is over. A CD-ROM project ends when the final master disc is delivered to the replicator. But Web sites are by their very nature dynamic and continuously updated (or they should be), so a Webmaster is generally a full-time employee who is devoted to continuous maintenance and upgrade.

Web sites may also employ producers, designers, and software engineers, but the Webmaster needs to be versed in all of these plus Web-specific procedures, programs, and languages such as HTML, Java, and ActiveX, which are used to create and maintain Web pages. Webmasters also need to be well-versed in computer networking technology, because part of the job may involve maintaining the physical equipment and connections that are required for a Web site, and in any case the Webmaster must coordinate with the systems administrator, who runs the network.

Often Webmasters must perform editorial functions, such as editing content or reviewing "Letters to the Editor" e-mail. Sometimes Webmasters are responsible for placing daily updated information on the Web site.

Where Do They Come From?   Webmasters may come from the ranks of programmers and interactive designers, and anyone who may have taught him or herself HTML and other skills related to the job. Because this is a relatively new field there is not much continuity with older jobs, except possibly for network engineers who have added HTML to their résumés.

Odd Jobs

There are many other possible jobs on an interactive project, depending on the nature of the material, the type of software used, and how much multimedia content is involved. There may be data managers who catalogue and arrange all of the text, graphics, and other multimedia assets; specialists in various programming languages; and musicians, narrators, recording engineers, and audio editors who create and refine the audio parts of a title.

Where Do They Come From?   In computer work, many people find that after they learn a specialized skill for a particular job, they are called upon to use that skill to perform similar tasks. Soon they find that they are considered expert in that job specialty. For example, they may find themselves doing data management or asset integration. This phenomenon is not limited to interactive media. Many experts in many disciplines have followed a similar career path. Of course, for many odd jobs, such as design management or audio engineering, more specific training is often required.

Subject Expert

Any title that covers a particular subject area (or many areas) should have one or more subject experts on the team. If a title is about gardening, for example, it helps to have someone on the team who knows something about horticulture. The subject expert not only provides guidance in editorial and nomenclature matters, but also possesses an insider perspective of the subject matter that can help determine the best interactive design. For example, subject experts know how the subject should be searched, so they can help design the searching procedures that are most appropriate for the title. They can also help design the organization or information architecture of the title. Subject experts also act as fact checkers to ensure the accuracy of the content.

Where Do They Come From?   Subject experts come from whatever field they are subject experts in. They may be from the academic world, or they can be doctors, lawyers, chefs, teaching and training experts, automobile mechanics, carpenters, or gardeners. In addition to the knowledge base they must have in their subject areas, they must be good communicators. Generally, this means that they have the ability to research and write in their area of expertise.

Writers and Editors

Last but certainly not least, all text, dialogue, narration, screen labels, and any miscellaneous text must be contributed by a writer. The text that appears onscreen must be edited and organized by an editor. There may be one or many writers on a project. In nonfiction and game titles, writers may have to create characters, situations, and dialogue in the same manner as screen and television writers. They must, however, have some experience and ability in dealing with the special needs of interactive writing. (Moreover, they should have read this book!)

Where Do They Come From?   Writers in the interactive media are writers first and foremost. They migrate to this field because they wish to expand their channels of communication to the interactive media. Sometimes this happens proactively, with the writer creating the opportunity; other times, the writer is asked to work on an interactive project. The type of writer most in demand for the new media is one who has written training manuals, videos, or games, or for corporate meetings, quiz shows, or, of course, any of the interactive media.

The Writer and Interactive Media

Writers are generally brought into a project in one of four ways:

- They are hired by the producer to write all or part of a title.
- They have written the original work on which the title is based.
- They submitted the idea to the publisher or producer and they want to adapt or develop it into a full-fledged interactive title.
- They have decided to write their own Web page or part of a Web site.

Have Word Processing Program, Will Travel

When writers are asked to write for the new media, they probably are known to the producer for having a particular skill set or style. Writers who are adept at creating scripts for training videos, writing questions for quiz shows, or writing for interactive corporate meetings, encyclopedia entries, advertising copy, and movie and television scripts are likely to be called upon to write all or part of an interactive title.

Writers who work for hire must be able to grasp the interactive structure of the title very quickly and to overcome the impulse to "just write." In interactive writing, structure is almost as important as content. Interactive media demands a short, self-contained format that differs from general-purpose writing. In some cases, the format and samples will be in place before the writer is brought in. The writer must follow this structure and supply the necessary information. The same holds true for interactive story-telling, in which the sections are generally shorter and more self-contained than in linear script writing.

Love My Book, Love Me

If you have written the print book on which an ebook is to be based, you may have a great deal to say about the organization and treatment of the interactive title. In this case, you will be involved before the structure and design are in place. You should be able to express your ideas about the interactive nature of the title and how it will be translated from the linear version. However, simply suggesting ideas for multimedia elements such as animation, audio, and video will not suffice. You must have a firm grasp of the nature of interactivity and what is likely to work and what won't. You might want to sketch out a flow diagram or storyboard along with a design or functional specification. A functional specification is a document that lists and describes the interactive features and explains how they relate to the content and to each other. Clearly, this kind of project control involves considerable work, but it is also quite satisfying.

On the other hand, writers should be aware that in many cases much less control is offered. Whether for legal, technical, or other reasons, many authors have little control over their work. For example, because of the large amount of information the new media can encompass, works from different authors are often combined in a single title. This can be distressing if the other works on the disc or online site are at variance with the author's sensibility, attitude, or philosophy.

We Love Your Idea: Let's Meet, and Bring Your Agent

You've got a bang-up, sure-fire idea for an interactive title and you've pitched it to a CD-ROM developer or online service and now they want to meet.

This scenario may be less likely to happen than the same scenario in the movie business, but it certainly does happen. In this case, the writer should endeavor to have as much involvement in the creative process as possible.

If you want to stay on top of the development of your idea, you should create the most detailed and thoroughly considered proposal that you possibly can. Interactive media are far more difficult to sketch out than a book proposal, magazine article query, or movie or television treatment. This is because editors and other decision makers in the traditional linear media can more easily envision the finished product. However, in the new media, it is more difficult to see the interactive layout and navigation until the title is actually produced. This is why many title developers insist on a *proof of concept* before committing to the project. A proof of concept may be a part of the actual title, created in a quick and dirty authoring program that can show a rudimentary version of the title with some of the interactivity actually functioning. In addition, it helps to have flowcharts, scripts, and detailed descriptions of every feature. It also helps to have drawings of some of the individual screens so that the idea can be better visualized by those who will make the final decision.

Legal Rights

In addition to creative, production, and technical issues, attention should be paid to legal issues in interactive title development.

The field of intellectual property law as it pertains to electronic publishing is relatively new and many of the fundamentals and business practices are still in development. For this reason, it is important for the writer to have access to an attorney who is well-versed in the very latest in this field. At the very least, the writer should have an agent who is familiar with electronic publishing. Many of the underlying principles in this field are not only new, but changing rapidly. Here are just a few of the questions writers need to ask:

- What are the going rates for writers of a Web site or a CD-ROM?
- How does one monitor sales of electronic media or hits to an online site?

- What is the customary royalty rate for media that can't be touched (media distributed in digital form)?
- What are the ramifications of international copyright law with regard to publishing on the World Wide Web?
- If I produce for my own Web site, do I control the rights to my work?
- What rights do I have if my work appears on a CD-ROM or Web site alongside another writer's work that contains ideas at odds with mine?

These are just some of the questions an agent or attorney familiar with this burgeoning field should be able to answer. We're sure you'll think of many more.

Summary

The writer is part of a creative production team which may include a producer, a design director, a software engineer, programmers, subject experts, Webmasters, and others as the project requires. The writer may be hired by the producer to write part of the project or may be brought in because the writer created the work on which the title is based. A writer may also create an original idea for an interactive title or online service or Web site and be hired to develop it.

The writer should have access to an attorney or agent who has experience with the new media and its legal and business practices. This field is new and constantly evolving, so the writer's representatives must stay in close touch with ongoing developments.

Part Two

Writing and Thinking
for Interactive Media

6

How to Think Interactively

Thought is an infection. In the case of certain thoughts, it becomes an epidemic.
—Wallace Stevens, poet

Free Association Training

The human mind is an interactive machine. We rarely think in a purely linear manner. To prove this, try an experiment: The next time you have the opportunity for uninterrupted thinking—while taking a walk by your-self or sitting in a park or waiting for a bus—pause your thoughts, and try to trace them back to their origin. If you can catch yourself in the middle of a thought, you will most likely see that some cue, such as a building, a street sign, children at play, or a random piece of overheard conversation, started the process, and you hyperlinked one thought to another until you settled on the most interesting or the most compelling one, which then occupied your mind.

Psychologists use this free association technique to help unlock deeply seated thoughts and emotions. They do this by instructing the subject to verbalize "the first thing that comes into your mind" in response to a word read aloud from a list. Of course, this provides only one hyperlink from the word on the list to the freely associated thought it provokes because the psy-chologist proceeds to the next word, which breaks the hyperlink from the previous free association. The process would be more interesting if you could continue to hyperlink on your own. In fact, you can try it and see what happens (when you're not being tested by a psychologist).

It is useful to consider the way the mind handles hyperlinking because an understanding of the mental mechanism can promote better interactive writing. The closer you can emulate the natural thought process, the easier it will be for your audience to follow the links and pat-terns. Moreover, retention will be much better.

Taming the Wandering Mind

The next time you read a book, try to catch yourself the first time you start thinking outside of the content of the text. Notice how many times and under what circumstances you begin to think of related (or unrelated) events and concepts that carry you away from the text you are reading (perhaps this is occurring at this very moment!). This happens to some people more than others and with some types of books more than others. It could be argued that the well-written content of a good book should not allow the reader's mind to wander; although this also depends on the reader, whose mind may wander no matter how the content is prepared. Even with the best-written material, some attentive readers will find themselves thinking either ahead in the subject matter or to related subject matter. Indeed, you could make the case that a book should actively stimulate associated thought.

Suppose that you are reading a book about the American Civil War. You bring to that reading experience some degree of familiarity with the subject matter. As you read about Gettysburg, for example, you might find yourself thinking about some associated material with which you are already familiar. Perhaps you have visited the battlefield. You might picture some of the settings you know in your mind as you read through a description of the battle. Or perhaps your great great great grandfather was an infantry officer who died during Pickett's Charge against the Union troops. Your oral family history, perhaps slightly embellished over time, might elicit an emotional response from you.

The point is that traditional, linear books can elegantly stimulate hyperlinking in the reader; indeed, that is the underlying power of any kind of storytelling, written or oral. However, for better or worse, with traditional media, readers must supply their own target links. If the writer of interactive material, either for CD-ROM or online, is attuned to the hyperlinking process, then efficient target links and sidebars can be written in anticipation of the reader. The interesting part of the task, of course, is to both guide and control the reader's thinking while allowing freely associated thought in the traditional manner. Perhaps that is essentially what makes the new media so interesting for both authors and users.

Summary

The exercises in this chapter suggest ways to make the writer aware of the mental process that accompanies hyperlinking, and they might help writers to think interactively. Although hyperlinking is potentially as unrestricted as daydreaming, writers must remain in charge of their interactive presentations, allowing freedom of thought yet guiding their readers through the subject matter.

By understanding this process, a writer can set up pathways that anticipate a reader's possible thought patterns and inclinations to take side trips, providing the reader with alternate pathways and side trips that efficiently add to the overall experience. In this way, the writer will gain greater control over the reader's attention and so will be able to maintain the reader's focus on the subject matter. Also, by anticipating the possible diversionary tugs at the reader's attention, the writer will be more effective in presenting the subject because there will be less chance for the reader to be distracted. Orwellian thought control, or expedient communication? You be the judge.

7

How to Choose
Interactive Content

Form and function are a unity, two sides of one coin. In order to enhance function, appropriate form must exist or be created.
                    —Ida P. Rolf, U.S. biochemist and physical therapist

Not everything in print must be interactive, nor will interactive media ever completely replace print. When television first burst upon the scene, the Hollywood film industry thought that the newer medium would be its downfall. Today, despite technological advances, we still have cinema as well as television, theater, radio, and recorded music. This is because different media serve different purposes. Radio has survived because it excels in situations in which listeners cannot watch a television screen (for example, while driving a car). The same is true for interactivity. It will not replace traditional media, and it shouldn't.

Earlier, we observed that paper books have certain built-in advantages and that these advantages should be retained in any interactive version. For an ebook to be successful, there must be a good reason to translate it from a paper book or to write it in the first place.

When Ebooks Don't Work

Here are some reasons why certain types of content don't translate well into interactive media:

- *The content doesn't benefit from interactive treatment.* Putting a book into interactive form should enhance it in some way. The mere fact that a reader needs an electronic device such as a com-

74

puter merely to read a book doesn't mean there is any benefit to be derived from it. In fact, if there is no enhancement as a result of the book's translation into an ebook, then it is likely that the value of the ebook will be *less* than the original print version. That an ebook's pages can be turned electronically, for example, does not add anything—you can turn the page as easily with a real book. Indeed, the tactile sensation of turning a physical page (not to mention licking your finger first) is a powerful one that is lost with an ebook.

- *There is too much screen-based reading.* In general, most people do not like to read large amounts of text from a computer screen. While many people spend much of their work time in front of a computer screen, they generally do not want to read long linear sections of material for enjoyment. Many readers even print out the material once they have located it electronically. Although our reading habits may very well change in the future, at least for now, predominantly text-based material (particularly fiction) is probably not a good choice for interactive adaptation.

- *The writer needs to maintain control over the content.* If the writer's skill lies primarily in presenting content with a unique style, that style may be adversely affected if the user has control over its organization. In fiction, the writer's ability to build character and plot may not translate well into a user-driven medium. A good mystery novel, for example, is successful predominantly because the plot is carefully directed. The solution to the mystery depends on the clues (obvious and otherwise) left by the writer. While it is possible to write an interactive mystery (and many writers have done so), the form has not caught on because once the writer yields control to the user, the writing skill is subordinated to the user's freedom to choose any of several possible outcomes. If several outcomes are possible, the inherent pleasure of a well-crafted mystery may be lost. The success of a few interactive mysteries is probably more a function of novelty than the writer's craft. Many other fiction styles don't translate for this same reason.

- *The primary purpose of the content is inspiration.* In some cases, the primary use for print material is to provide inspiration or stimulate ideas on the part of the user through random browsing. A book of photographs may provide inspiration to an artist. A fashion magazine may give people ideas for their wardrobe. In fact, most catalogues are designed for browsing. Interactivity may add useful features, such as the ability to change the color of an object, or to help organize the content, but if the content is primarily browse-oriented, then the benefits of translating it into an electronic format must be seriously considered because the ability to randomly browse is an intuitive function that is generally best handled in print. The World Wide Web, of course, uses software "browsers" to access its content, and these are becoming more useful for inspiration because of the sheer amount of information available. The availability of all the issues of a magazine or newspaper in one location makes this sort of browsing more useful in electronic form than in print. However, because print allows more intimate physical contact with the material, it still has an edge over the browsability of electronic media. It should be noted, however, that this issue is somewhat controversial, and the position stated here is not universally held.

- *There is not enough portability.* Even small notebooks and handheld computers are not as portable as a paperback book. Linear material that is designed to be read in many locations (perhaps on the beach or a camping trip) should be left to the printed page. Regular books don't need batteries or a wall outlet.

When Ebooks Do Work

Here are some reasons why certain types of material translate well into interactive media:

- *It benefits from hyperlinking.* Any time hyperlinking improves the content, the ebook is very likely to be an improvement over the print version. For example, the ability to drill down through large volumes of data or skip from one database to another is expedited by hyperlinking.

- *It benefits from nonlinearity.* If the content is better expressed when the order of access can be determined by the user, then it is a good prospect for interactive adaptation or treatment. An ebook about house-building benefits from the ability to look at the section on electrical wiring without having to fast forward through the section on pouring the concrete foundation.
- *It benefits from the addition of multimedia.* If the content would benefit from the user hearing something such as music or pronunciations, or seeing something such as the Heimlich maneuver, then these elements linked to text would make the ebook more useful than a print book or a videotape.
- *It benefits from data density.* If a 24-volume encyclopedia can be placed on a single CD-ROM disc, the benefits can be measured in shelf space alone. This also enhances portability and decreases cost.
- *It benefits from searching.* If the usefulness of the content is enhanced by the ability of the user to locate any piece of information, or to access any hierarchical section instantly, it is a good candidate for an ebook.

Does MIT Have the Answer?

As we have seen, when we improve certain content by converting it to interactive media we lose some of the inherent benefits of books. If we have instant hyperlinking, then we lose the book's tactile qualities and portability. Perhaps the answer to the dilemma of marrying the touchy-feely qualities of books with the advantages of interactive media is to have it both ways. According to Nicholas Negroponte of the MIT Media Lab, there is an electronic product in the works that has flexible pages that can be turned and leafed through like a book, but whose content is supplied through digital electronic cartridges or data uploads. The pages have a display capability similar to that used in notebook computer screens. This ebook device looks and feels somewhat like a book but has many of the advantages of digital interactive media.

This entire concept may seem ludicrous to those of us who think there is nothing wrong with the smell of paper and printer's ink, but the fact that a device like this is even under consideration points up the dilemma of interactivity: How do we improve on the book without losing its many benefits?

Summary

Content that is destined to be a good ebook will be more useful, more accessible, and more dynamic than its noninteractive counterpart while preserving as many of the positive characteristics of a traditional print book as possible. However, when determining what will work best as an interactive title, it is important to realize that the decision may not be obvious. More than likely, when ascertaining suitability for interactivity, the content under consideration will generate both pros and cons. Writers should ask themselves how converting existing content into an interactive title, or writing an original ebook instead of a print book, will have added value to the user. At the same time, the writer must consider such issues as the loss of portability, the need for a playback device, and the loss of the physical possession of a book. If it is determined that there is a distinct advantage to presenting the content interactively, then chances are good that the result will be a very useful or entertaining title.

8

How to Plan and Present an Interactive Title Idea

Measure twice; cut once.
> —Norm Abram, Master Carpenter (and others before him)

Sometimes a writer is called upon to add components to an existing interactive CD-ROM or online title. Other times the writer might create an entirely new interactive title. The latter calls for organizational discipline if it is to be completed successfully. In this chapter, we shall describe a three-phase plan for original title creation. Phase I covers planning an interactive title; Phase II shows how to present a treatment or proposal to a developer or publisher; and Phase III details the procedure for writing an interactive title.

Phase I: Planning an Interactive Title

The first step in planning an interactive title is quite similar to planning a linear title: The writer must decide on the title's audience and focus. In addition, the writer must determine the platform for the electronic delivery of the title. There are many different types of computers in use today, but in general writers need be concerned only with PCs and Macs. We'll defer technical details until Chapter 23, which discusses computer platforms. The writer must also know whether the title is to be distributed via a physical medium such as CD-ROM or floppy disc, or online over the World Wide Web or an online service. Here, we'll focus on choosing the audience (Chapter 21 discusses online and CD-ROM distribution and their special concerns.)

Choosing an audience for a new title is somewhat more difficult than with traditional writing because there are so many more variables. Here is a list of questions about the audience that the writer should be able to answer before starting to write an interactive title:

- *What is the level of computer literacy of the average user?* The answer to this question will help the writer determine the com- plexity of the organization of the information and what features will be needed. It will also help the writer determine how much navigation and user help will have to be written. Experienced users learn how to navigate quickly, but they are also more likely to expect organization and layout to conform to their previous experience. It should be noted that computer literacy is increasing exponentially and will become less of an issue to writers in years to come.
- *What familiarity does the audience have with the subject matter?* This is much more difficult to determine than with a traditional linear title because various degrees of familiarity might be assumed on a single disc. Clearly, for widest audience appeal, multiple information depths should be provided for different users. Unlike traditional media, interactive media provides this unique capability: The same title can aim at a wide variety of user sophistication levels without any user being adversely affected.
- *Will the audience access this title on disc or online?* Both discs and online services have advantages and disadvantages that must be considered. Discs have a fixed (though large) capacity (sometimes called disc *real estate*). Discs provide instant gratification because they can provide users with access to complex multimedia data quickly. However, discs need a relatively long lead time from finished production to distribution to the user. On the other hand, content distribution on the Web and other online systems can be as immediate as the time it takes to write it. In addition, with the Web and online systems distribution is automatic, with every computer in the world capable of accessing it immediately. However, current online systems tend to be less capable of handling multimedia efficiently. Depending on the connection, audio files may not play immediately after being accessed, and the slower the connection, the lower the quality of the sound. Video online is even more problematic—for reasonably high quality, it must be downloaded to the user's

computer in its entirety before it can be seen, and this time lag can be substantial; it often takes twenty minutes to a half hour before one minute of video can be viewed. All of this is changing rapidly, but the principles are consistent. The higher the quality of the audio or video, the more difficult it is to get it to the online user. A disc provides capacity; an online service provides immediacy. Neither (as yet) provides both.

- *Where is this title most likely to be used (at home, in a library, in school, while traveling)?* The answer to this question can help the writer determine how much multimedia material the title should contain. For example, many libraries prefer not to have multimedia on their computers because the audio can be disturbing to others and headphones are difficult to maintain. To a lesser extent, the user's likely environment can have an impact on writing style. For example, a travel guide designed for on-the-road should have short, easy-to-locate sections. Conversely, a travel guide designed to be read at home or in a library might have larger sections of text or background information.

- *What type of computer system will be used to access the title?* This will have an impact on the system's ability to play and display multimedia (especially video), the amount of text and pictures that can be displayed with reasonable speed, and even the ability to perform a search effectively. Also, different computer systems have somewhat different navigation controls and require different screen layouts.

After answering these questions, the writer should begin to organize the material and contemplate how the interactivity will enhance the presentation of the content. At the same time, the nature of the multimedia elements (called *assets*) should be considered. This leads to another set of questions the writer must answer:

- *What interactive features will be used in the title?* This group is called the feature set, and it is key to the development of any interactive title. Hierarchical navigation, hyperlinking, searching, and multimedia issues all should be addressed before one word is written because the use of these features determines what is written and how it is written. Writers should think about whether the user will be allowed to print out all or part of the content; whether there will be a copy-and-paste feature that allows the user to copy content from the title and paste it into a word processing program; or whether there will be other interactive features, such as games, in the title.

- *Will the title require any special programming?* Any feature that goes beyond typical hyperlinking and multimedia may require special programming. These features can include drag-and-drop capability (in which the mouse or other pointing device is used to move icons, text, and/or other images to another part of the screen where they activate some program function); the ability to launch another application; any type of hand-eye game play; random generation of text, images, or audio; creation of search engines; or any other process the computer may be called upon to perform that does not fall under the category of basic hyperlinking and multimedia functions.

- *Should multimedia be employed?* Writers sometimes conceptualize an entire title and then realize that they have left out multimedia. Realizing that multimedia is important, they add it as an afterthought. If a title works without multimedia, authors probably should not add it. Publishers may disagree, feeling that it is necessary to have multimedia for marketing purposes. They may be right, but it doesn't enhance a title. For example, music that plays behind unrelated text can be annoying. Having a voice-over of the same text that is on the screen is often intrusive and counter to the effectiveness of the title unless the title is designed for sight-impaired or preschool users. Multimedia must be planned as carefully as text. It should be chosen to illustrate what cannot be expressed in print, and it must be designed to be accessed in an intuitive manner. Multimedia can be very expensive in both fees and royalties. Writers should research the sources for multimedia; both publishers and developers will want to know the owners of the music, animation, video clips, and so on.

- *How will multimedia elements be deployed?* As with a traditional print title, the writer must determine how photographs and illustrations are to be used. The writer must also determine how audio, video, and animation will be used if any of them will be included. In any case, the writer must deal with rights issues. The writer should establish exactly how each multimedia element will be used and how the user will access it. Audio and video can be played in many ways: Segments can automatically start playing when a user accesses a hyperlink, they can be played only upon a direct choice made by the user, or they can be linked to many other possible conditions set by the programming. However they are accomplished, it is not enough for a writer simply to say "We'll have speeches by the major historical figures" or "We'll have some video of each country." The writer must know how these multimedia elements will be seen or heard by the user and how they will be related (if at all). Writers don't have to map out the entire title; they only have to indicate how each asset is going to be presented and the relation each has to the others. Once this has been accomplished, the writer can get down to the task of writing the title.

Phase II: The Presentation—How to Present Your Title to a Developer or Publisher

A proposal for an interactive title need not contain every hyperlink and every feature to be found in the completed work. Interactivity is like a game of chess. The rules seem deceptively simple, but after a few moves, play can become extremely complex. For this reason, no experienced developer or publisher expects to see every permutation of the functionality of a title. But they do expect to see the basic relationship between the content and the interactive features. As with a book proposal, the more complete it is, the better the chance it will be interpreted properly and accepted. A proposal for an interactive ebook title should contain the following sections:

- *Overview or executive summary.* This is a brief abstract; from this section the publisher and developer can get a sense of what the proposal is about. It should describe the content and the way the interactive features will be used.

- *Description of objectives.* This section should contain a discussion of the marketing elements, such as product positioning, the tone, the target audience, and the approach to the user interface. If the title is intended for online delivery, a description of the business model should be included as well, because online titles can be advertiser-supported, subscription-based, or paid for on a per-use basis. Because a large proportion of the online universe is free to the user, the writer should keep in mind that the publisher/developer needs to derive revenue directly or indirectly from the publication of the title.

- *Detailed summary of the title.* This is where the writer describes the title in detail. The user interface should be described, along with the navigation system, the organization, and the presentation of the content. This section should take the developer through the title so that every aspect is clear.

- *Flowcharts.* The flow of the navigation should be diagrammed in some detail. The main functional areas should be shown so that the developer can see how the user accesses the content. The navigational flow is the road map for the layout of the content. The writer must first understand how the content is to be organized and how the user will access it. This is done by deciding upon the types of content to be included in the title.

- *Screen diagrams.* The writer need not be an artist, but screen diagrams are necessary for any interactive title proposal. Because the success of an interactive title may depend as heavily on the presentation of the content as the content itself, the writer will need to provide a preliminary blueprint for screen layout along with the other elements of the proposal. Screen diagrams show the general use of the user's screen area; that is, what the user sees in terms of the types of information, the layout, navigational controls, and so forth. The main screen shows what the user sees when the title starts. It is often the home base from which all exploration is launched. How much of the screen is devoted to text, pictures, and controls will determine not only the title's aesthetics but its ease of use.

- *Description of the product feature set.* Every important feature in the title should be described in detail. These can include special uses of maps; specific uses of audio, such as pronunciations for a language title; interactive glossary; database organization; the ability to print out sections of text or pictures; tutorials; user customization (for example, a title on gardening could display blooming cycles for plants keyed to the user's geographical location); scrapbooks that allow the user to collect data throughout the title for later printing or copying into a word processing program; help features; and so on.

- *Analysis of assets.* The writer should list all image, audio, video, and animation assets and specify whether they will need to be licensed from outside sources. If photographs must be researched and fees negotiated, this information should be included here along with names of the specific rights-holding organizations. For example, if you are writing about baseball and you expect to include some video footage of the 1969 World Series, you should be able to identify the ball club or television network that holds the rights.

- *Budget (optional).* While it is not necessary for the writer to provide a budget, it may be helpful. Promising numbers may persuade the developer or publisher of the feasibility of producing the title for a cost that makes sense in relation to its prospective revenue. Writers won't lose any points, however, if they omit this item, because developers and publishers will most likely want to prepare their own cost estimates.

Phase III: How to Plan to Write a Title

Many writers begin a book or article by writing an outline. Outlines are good for planning interactive titles as well, but they don't go far enough. Outlines by their very nature are hierarchical, and they are useful for getting the ideas down. However, to lay out the interactive relationships, the best approach is to prepare a flowchart. This can be done in longhand on a piece of paper or it can be done using flowcharting software, as described in Chapter 9.

Writers should begin the process by imagining the user sitting in front of a screen. What is the first thing the user sees? In a paper book, it might be the table of contents, the preface, or the introduction—there are also the title and copyright pages, but readers usually skip them. In an interactive title, it is important that the navigation means through the title be presented on the main screen. There may be preliminary screens (often called splash screens) before the main screen, but these are similar to the title pages and other front matter of a book—they are not part of the main body of the work. The main screen functions as a home base in an interactive title. It also acts as a hyperlinked table of contents, with each chapter or section heading linked to its content. Not only is it a point of departure, but it is a place to return to after reading, listening, or viewing other parts of the title so that further navigation can be accomplished.

An example of a flowchart is shown in Figure 8.1. The main screen is the box at the top. The next level of the flowchart shows the first level of the hierarchy. If this were a linear book, these would be the chapters. If the chapters were arranged in parts or sections, the boxes on this level would represent those divisions.

The writer should also determine the tools the user will need on the various screens: Search, help, print, and the navigation controls (go back, quit, and so on) are all tools that may or may not appear on every screen. Tools can also consist of other specialized features that are designed for the specific title. It is important not to confuse tools with the navigational flow of the title.

In our French Revolution title, the writer may wish to present the main information in chronological chunks. Biographical information may be presented in pop-up windows, it can be put in sidebars that the user can access by clicking on a name in a chronological chunk, or it may be put into a separate section altogether, with links back to the chronological section.

It is important for writers to be more aware of the design of an ebook than they would be were they writing traditional linear material. In print, writers can write without any notion of how the book or magazine article will be laid out (of course the editor may call for a few sidebars, but they are treated as separate although related material). In an ebook, the functionality is so intertwined with the content that the writer cannot simply write and ignore the interactivity.

The process of actually writing an interactive title is just one of many tasks facing the writer. Writers may find that they spend equal amounts of time writing, researching, sketching, and creating flowcharts.

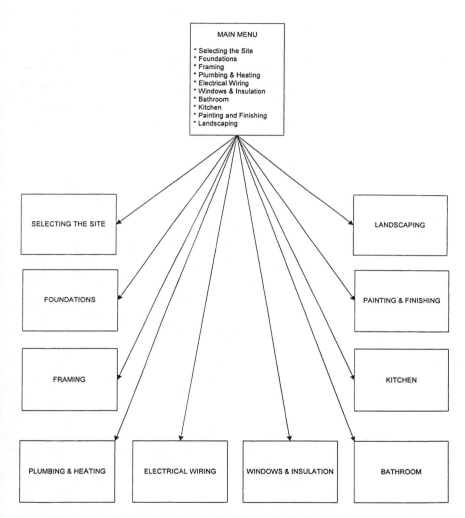

Figure 8.1 A top level flowchart for a title called *How to Build a House*. As we can see, the main menu shows the topics as a table of contents would in a linear book. Each box represents that topic's top-level menu item. The flowchart would continue on, with each topic becoming the top level of its own section. Each section would have its own subheadings. By using basic navigational tools, which would appear on each screen such as Go Forward, Go Back, and Go to Main Menu, the user can navigate the entire title interactively using the Main Menu screen as a home base.

Although the process described here applies more to a CD-ROM title than to a Web site, the creation of a good Web site will have most of the same proposal and planning tasks. Many software programs that allow Web authors to visualize the hierarchical relationships of their pages and the interrelationships of individual links throughout a site are available. These organization programs are highly recommended to Web authors, particularly for larger sites. Because writers may be either creating an entire CD-ROM or Web site or just contributing to either, the planning may or may not be very elaborate.

Summary

In planning an interactive title, the writer needs to address many issues before actually beginning to write. Is the title well-suited to an interactive presentation? What multimedia assets would be suitable? After making these important assessments, the writer must pitch the title to a developer and address issues such as objectives, content, general design, and cost. Once the job is secured, the writer may use an outline to get the main ideas down on paper, but should also create a flow diagram showing the layout of the information in the title.

9

Tools to Help Develop Your Ideas and Plan the Title

Can it core a apple?

—Ed Norton on *The Honeymooners*

When you begin work on an interactive title, it will quickly become apparent that you'll need a few more tools beyond your trusty word processor. We've already discussed the necessity of flowcharting a new title, so we'll begin by looking at flowcharting software.

Flowcharting Software

You can draw flowcharts freehand if you wish, but they probably won't be very presentable and may become confusing as you cross out and redraw. Flowcharting software lets the writer experiment with different pathways and allows you to move the boxes representing screens and processes on your screen. Most of these programs will draw the connecting lines automatically, which is a big help if you've ever tried to do this using a pen and ruler. But the best part of such a program is the ability to undo and re-create any box, label, or connecting line. Cut, copy, and paste functions are as useful in flowcharting software as they are in word processors. Many of these packages also offer predesigned chart types, or templates, from which the writer can choose to suit the particular title at hand.

Whatever type of flowchart the writer selects, it is a good idea to label each level according to a hierarchical numbering system. Figure 9.1 shows an example of this system.

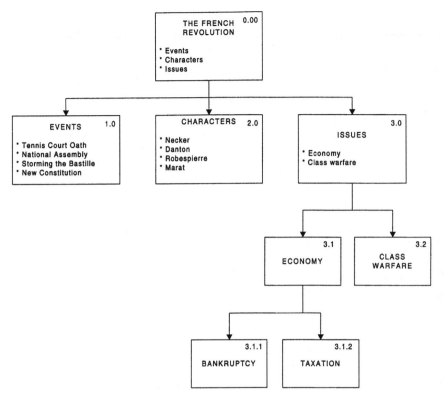

Figure 9.1 This partial flowchart for a title on the French Revolution shows a hierarchical numbering system using decimal notation. The first level of the Main Menu numbers each area using incremental whole digits (1,2,3, etc.). Each subheading uses a decimal to indicate its relationship to its parent in the hierarchy (1.1, 1.2, 1.3, etc.) The parent's number is retained for each subsequent level and the decimal is added with incremental increases on the decimal level for each item on the same level.

This is only one system of numbering. Any hierarchical system, such as those used in outlining, can be used. The advantage of the type shown here is that its numbers can be used to program the links and sequences in a programming language, which requires numbers rather than letters. Some programs used for interactive media cannot use the decimals, however, and programmers may remove them. Then they may add zeros in order to keep the number of digits for each box uniform.

Word Processing Programs

Beyond their obvious function as a writing tool, many word processors offer the ability to hyperlink within a document. This feature can be invaluable in trying out links between ideas. In addition, the major word processing programs offer the ability to embed or link *objects*, or media, from other programs within the word processing document. This system, called *OLE (Object Linking and Embedding)* allows the writer to experiment with hypermedia links by linking an audio or video clip to a word or phrase within a word processing document. This can be extremely useful for checking the basic interactive flow of a multimedia title.

Most of the major word processing programs allow writers to create documents that will display properly in a Web browser. Using these programs, writers can create Web pages as easily as they create word processed documents. Linking a word or section of text internally within the document, or externally to an entirely different location on the Internet, is as easy as making a word bold or italic. In some cases, creating a Web page is as simple as clicking on the option that says Save as HTML. Writers can also use contemporary word processing software to insert pictures and sounds into a document that can be displayed on the World Wide Web.

Drawing and Painting Programs

Depending on the writer's level of computer graphic capability, a drawing or painting program may be useful in testing visual ideas. The main difference between these two program types is that drawing programs (often called vector graphic programs) deal with lines and shapes and posterlike fills, while painting programs (often called bitmap or photo editing programs) can be used to create more photographic images. For diagramming, drawing programs are more useful. If you need to work with photographic images, a painting package will be more useful. Of course, there is some overlap and each program can handle the other type of art to a lesser degree.

More elaborate (and more expensive) painting programs offer a layering feature that can be useful to the writer who wishes to test out interactive screen designs. The writer can create a screen design, then overlay it with subsequent screen designs that utilize elements of the first. By turning these layers on and off, the writer can see the effect of clicking on a button and going to the next level in the hierarchy of the title.

Writers needn't be concerned if they don't possess graphic ability. But if they do, these software packages can help them to visualize their interactive ideas realistically.

Interactive Authoring Programs

For writers who wish to test their interactive ideas in an almost finished form, there is a wide variety of authoring programs that run the ease-of-use gamut from beginner to rocket scientist. Some of the fairly basic authoring programs essentially combine elements of flowcharting, word processing, and graphics programs. Elements can be easily programmed to link and initiate interactive routines when the user clicks the mouse on a hot spot. However, like all software, these programs follow the usability rule that says that the easier a program is to use, the less it can accomplish.

At the other end of the spectrum are the feature-rich authoring programs that are used by programmers to create professional commercial titles. These programs, like Macromedia's Director, can be used by beginners, but most of their power lies in a complex programming language that carries with it a steep learning curve for the more advanced (and even some of the basic) features. For example, if you wish to include a search engine in your title, you'll have to know a bit about programming in addition to the fundamental interactive and multimedia functions of the program.

Simple programs can be useful to writers if they just want to test out their ideas. Although more sophisticated programs allow great depth of presentation, some authors may find that they are spending more time figuring out the program than writing the title they originally set out to create. Ultimately, the choice of an authoring program is an individual decision.

Presentation Programs

Presentation programs are used for business presentations in a slide show format. But the more sophisticated of these programs offer hyperlinking and basic animation, which can be useful in creating simple interactive programs. While the programs can help writers get the feel of the interactivity conceptualized for an interactive title, they are generally too limited to be useful beyond the most basic interactivity. For example, they offer limited text scrolling capability and cannot perform any searches.

Programming Languages

In the unusual but fortuitous circumstance that the writer is also a programmer, a programming language may be used to create all or part of an interactive title. These languages deal with the computer on a fundamental level, issuing instructions to the operating system and sometimes directly to the hardware to accomplish their tasks. In general, this approach is not a good one for the writer because testing and prototyping simply takes too long. But if the writer happens to be a skilled programmer, it may be possible to achieve results that would otherwise be unattainable.

Programs to Help the Writer Stay Organized

Although a word processing program can accomplish many of the tasks of organization, such as keeping and sorting lists, it may be useful for a writer to employ a dedicated database program to keep track of assets, documents, files, and so on. There are many database programs on the market, and they tend to be relatively easy to use. If they are set up well, the writer can easily keep track of the source of each picture, for example, along with its copyright information, location, status, availability, license fees, and photographer's or artist's credit information. The earlier in the project such databases are set up, the less crazed the writer is likely to become later on.

Summary

Writers should take advantage of many of the software programs that can help them add interactivity to their titles. Word processors often contain features that allow the writer to experiment with hyperlinking, hypermedia, and online ideas. Drawing and painting programs can help the writer visualize screen design. Authoring programs can help the writer test out interactivity in a title, and database programs are very useful for organizing resources during the development of an interactive title.

10

Planning for Interactivity in a Linear Title

In preparing for battle I have always found that plans are useless, but planning is indispensable.

—Dwight D. Eisenhower

Let's say you are working on a book, magazine article, or other traditional print-destined material and you believe you might one day want to turn your work (or at least part of it) into an interactive title. Can you write in the linear realm with an eye toward the world of hyperlinks? The answer depends, of course, on the type of material you're working on. Some types of material translate better into interactive works than others. Nonfiction, in particular, can be written in a way that anticipates conversion into non-linearity. Specifically, it would be a good idea to keep the following in mind:

- Organize your material into smaller sections than you ordinarily would. Nonlinear writing is much better if it allows the user to link freely from concept to concept. Sometimes it can be very difficult to structure your work on a print title in this way, but the nature of nonlinearity demands that you attempt it. Moreover, if you try to write so that each section functions as independently as possible it sometimes forces you to rethink the organization of a piece, and that process can be beneficial for both the current print version and the interactive version that will follow.
- Write background material so that later it can be hyperlinked to foreground material. In other words, try to write so that the background material does not necessarily have to flow in a specific order within the main text. Once again, forcing you to think more critically about organization can benefit both the print and the interac-

tive versions. If possible, try to write in levels. The foreground narrative should link events, topics, or concepts, while the background functions to enhance the information by giving examples, providing context, or offering explanations to readers who bring different levels of knowledge to the subject.

- Use glossaries, lists, timelines, bibliographies, short biographical sketches, and so on. In a print article, these elements, placed in sidebars, can enhance the main piece. In the interactive version, they can be linked to the main piece in pop-up boxes and other such devices.

- Create examples that can be specifically adapted to use multimedia later. When the title becomes nonlinear, it can use audio and video to illustrate important points. It is important that the writer consider these elements while writing the print version. That way, they will integrate much more realistically when they are finally used. Otherwise, they may look like they were added just to beef up the title.

Summary

If you write a linear title that you might want to convert into an interactive one, think in terms of tight organization. Whereas the print writer must think about the development of themes and overall structure, the interactive writer needs to think primarily about organization. Thinking about organization means that you consider layers and interrelationships between the parts in addition to the structure of the whole. Sometimes it is possible to follow a dual path to a print article and an interactive one, but much material destined for print often cannot be forced into an interactive organization. Even when this is the case, writing with an eye toward interactivity is still a good exercise because it forces you to examine the structure and organization of the material. In some cases, the exercise of considering the work from two different standpoints will stimulate better thinking, and hence better writing.

Part Three

Interactive Grammar—
The Parts of Interactive Speech

11

The Grammar of Interactivity

Stay right here, 'cause these are the good old days.
—Carly Simon (From "Anticipation")

From primitive origins, interactive media is beginning to evolve into a sophisticated means of expression. This progression is similar to the evolution of film. The technology of moving pictures evolved into the art form of cinema because a well-defined grammar developed that allowed the medium to express a rich tapestry of ideas, emotions, actions, plot, subtext, drama, and theme. This grammar evolved gradually over many years, with experimentation and new technology adding more and more to film's syntax.

Cinematic Grammar

In the early days of film, simple elements of film grammar such as close-ups, medium shots, and soundtrack music were unthinkable. Early film-makers thought audiences would be horrified if a person were to be framed in any other way than a full head-to-toe shot because they reasoned that audiences would think the person had been cut in half. It took time for filmmakers to feel comfortable using various shot framings and camera angles to tell their stories. In fact, early filmed drama consisted of a single shot of a stage play from beginning to end, and the filming would pause only when the reel in the camera had to be changed. Likewise, when audio technology was introduced, it wasn't until the time of David O. Selznick (the 1930s) that most filmmakers realized it was permissible to have a soundtrack that featured recorded music without causing audience members to wonder where the orchestra was.

Filmmakers eventually learned to overcome these naive assumptions and began to develop a serious grammar that allowed them to construct scenes with master shots, medium shots, and close-ups, and to create montages that showed concurrent activity in different locations, creating a sense of intensifying emotion. For example, film buffs will recall that montage was mastered by Sergei Eisenstein in the Odessa Steps sequence from his *Battleship Potemkin* (1925), in which the juxtaposition of shots of marching troops, steel bayonets, fleeing crowds, weeping mothers, and a careening baby carriage creates a powerful emotion. Filmmakers also developed other types of montages to show the passage of time and changing emotion. For example, in *Citizen Kane* (1941) Orson Welles showed the deterioration of the lead character's marriage over time by cutting together shots of the increasingly estranged couple moving farther and farther apart in breakfast scenes from many different mornings over a period of several years.

It pays to look at a mature medium such as film because it may help us to understand these early days of interactive media. The grammar here is certainly not mature, and years of evolution will be required until the new media are fully developed. Because the new media will be used for many different purposes and will be delivered over many different distribution systems, the development of interactive grammar is likely to be far more complex than that of film. But even now, we have accumulated enough experience to begin examining this grammar. It is important that we do this now so that writers will be able to understand the fundamentals of interactive media with as much authority as they have in the traditional media.

Since the new media combine many art forms—from text writing to film, television, and radio—it might seem difficult to base a grammatical structure on just one of these. But because we see interactive media as an outgrowth of language, we shall develop our theory of interactive grammar around the nomenclature of the grammar of language.

Interactive Nouns and Verbs

Any tutorial discussion of grammar must begin with the most fundamental language elements. In western language we employ nouns and verbs.

We all learned, perhaps rather painfully, that nouns are things and verbs are actions. This holds pretty much true for interactive media. The things are the assets or elements: words, pictures, video, audio, and so on. In interactive media, these things are not by themselves interactive. When you display text, for example, it remains static on the screen. You read it noninteractively. The same holds true for images, static or moving, and for audio. The verbs, on the other hand, are the actions: Click, drag and drop, and draw are all actions the user can take. These are the elements that make interactive media truly interactive. When you combine interactive nouns and verbs, you create interactive content. When you create a flowchart for an interactive title, you are in effect laying out relationships between nouns and verbs—in fact, you are diagramming an interactive sentence.

The Elements of Interactive Grammar

Nouns are not particularly exciting when we talk about interactivity in the abstract. Of course, they define the content of an interactive title. But the elements that make it all happen are the verbs. Here's where the user takes control and moves it all into the interactive realm. In other words, that's where the fun really begins. The following inventory of current interactive verbs shows us the state of the art.

Hyperlinks: Iverbs Connecting Inouns

From the grammatical standpoint, hyperlinks are verbs embedded in nouns. A piece of text (the noun) may contain a hyperlink (the verb). Clicking on the hyperlink produces the action that may lead to another noun (more text). Or a picture may contain hot spots that link to another picture, or to some text, or to a multimedia element. In each case, the hyperlink or hot spot is the verb, which links one noun to another. And these verbs are found inside interactive nouns. We will cleverly call these interactive nouns *inouns* to distinguish them from the traditional use of these terms in linear grammar. Likewise, we will call our interactive verbs *iverbs* to set them apart from traditional grammar as well.

Clearly, interactive media have a relationship to the grammar of text and speech, but interactive media also have a relationship to the complex grammar of film. Film grammar involves the juxtaposition of visual elements that creates an emotional response in the viewer that could not be created by any of the elements alone. An example of this that is widely cited in film schools is a shot of a man's face. His expression is neutral. The next shot shows a plate of food. Then the two shots are cut together. When they see the shots together, most students will infer that the man is hungry. In interactive media a similar relationship exists between iverbs and inouns. When it is done correctly, both the design environment and the visual placement can have an important emotional and intellectual impact on the user.

In an interactive presentation, hyperlinks are usually indicated so that the user knows where to click. In text, the link may be set off by type that differs in color from the rest of the text. In a picture, the hot spot may be set off from the background by a border, a different color background, or some automatic action such as instantly displaying clarifying text or pictures when pointed to (see *rollover* later). The term *hot spot* is generally used when referring to a clickable area of a picture; hot link and hyperlink, which both mean the same thing, refer to a part of a picture or text that, when clicked, links to another part of the title or produces additional text, image, or audio material. In many cases, hot spots are identified when the cursor changes shape; for example, a cursor arrow may change into a hand with a pointing finger.

The manner in which hyperlinks and hot spots are presented determines the psychological and intellectual state the user will be in when the link jumps to its object (we say when the link *resolves* itself). If a link is clearly marked—for example, the text is highlighted in a different color— the user assumes that the link is important, perhaps even fundamental to the main concept in the section of text being viewed. But if the link is not set off from the rest of the text it must be discovered, and the user may infer that it is not particularly essential. In fact, the user may not notice the link at all.

Sometimes all the words in a given piece of text will be hyperlinks, so that the user can find the definition of any word. In some encyclopedias, for example, every word is a hot link except *stop words* (words such as "a," "the," "and," and "if.") In this case, the user knows that every word will be defined when it is clicked. This creates a uniform expectation level for the user: All words produce the same level of elaboration when clicked. There is thus no need to highlight all the words in another color—that would have the effect of creating *de facto* highlighting for the stop words, which would be the only words *not* highlighted. This would be similar to printing an entire book in boldface type.

However, if only certain words are highlighted, then the user has a heightened sense of expectation towards each hyperlink, because they are relatively scarce. These hyperlinks may take the user to a totally different area of the title, or, in the case of online media, to a different computer in a different country.

It is possible, of course, to use multiple colors or fonts to delineate different kinds of hyperlinks, but that tends to interfere with the title's general typography. In general, the user will understand that a particular color denotes a hot link, while text in other colors or fonts is used in the same way as it is in traditional media—for design and emphasis.

If a picture has hidden hot spots, the way they are marked implies their level of importance. For example, if a picture contains several hot spots, they may be set off by a border or some graphic element; or a graphic effect such as the color changing or inverting; or a sound effect; or the display of a previously hidden border or other graphic might be triggered by the cursor entering the hot spot's boundaries. The hot spots might not be marked at all. In each of these cases, a different message is sent to the user about the importance or use of the hot spot. To summarize the ways in which hot spots can be presented, and what their impact is on the user, here is a short list:

- *Set off by an always visible border.* The user sees the hot spots clearly and does not have to discover them. If the writer wants the user to know unambiguously that there are hot spots available, and that they are represented in the graphic image by clearly delineated areas, the user will infer a high level of importance for the links. Inexperienced users will be more likely to access them.
- *Set off by inverting color, changing shape or color, or by a sound effect, when the cursor moves into the boundary.* This is a much more discovery-dependent way of communicating the existence of

the hot spot in a graphic. It requires that the user discover it by search or by accident.

- *Not set off in any way.* If all of the hot spots are hidden, the user must guess whether and where to click in order to find them. This approach can be used in children's activity titles, where several hot spots are hidden for the child to discover. In this case, the links will produce an immediate and local event such as the playing of a sound or the initiation of animation. But hidden hot spots are generally not very effective as a tool for writers, who usually want the hot spots to be seen and known in advance by the user. Except in special cases, hiding hot spots usually has little value and works against the user's emotional tie to the material.

It is clear that the grammar of hyperlinks and hot spots will be a major area of study for future interactive grammarians. What we have hoped to demonstrate is that there is already a basis for determining how iverbs function within the interactive framework. Understanding their emotional and intellectual impact on the user is part of the fundamental grammar of interactive media.

Pop-Ups

When a hyperlink is clicked, it can produce a short selection of text, usually in a box, which superimposes over the screen and provides information related to the subject. Pop-ups are usually used to provide a definition or other short support information. They can appear when the mouse enters the hyperlink's hot spot, or they can appear only when clicked on. Pop-ups can remain on the screen until the user performs some action, such as another click, or they may stay on the screen only while the mouse button remains held down. All of these actions and states determine the impact of a pop-up:

- *Pop-up appears when the cursor enters the hot spot.* This action is often called a *rollover* because the pop-up message appears when the cursor rolls over the hot spot and stays on screen as long as the cursor stays there. This is the most discoverable of all pop-up appearance triggers. Users will find a definition or other useful information related to the hyperlink without having to take any overt action. It is, however, somewhat intrusive because users have little control over it (in some programs, pop-ups can be disabled).

Rollovers are often used in applications programs such as word processors and spreadsheets to identify the functions of the icons that provide various features. If a user is unfamiliar with the functions of some icons, it is useful to be able to answer "what's this?" by simply pointing to an icon or word. Because applications programs require that users click or double-click on the icon to activate a program feature, clicking on the icon to find out what the feature is or what it does is not possible. Therefore, this function works instead as a rollover. Sometimes these rollovers are shaped like the speech balloons from comic strips, which is why they are sometimes called *balloon help*.

In other types of interactive material, rollovers must be used sparingly because they are the least interactive form of pop-up. However, they can be very useful in cases where the writer wants the user to have handy reference to many hyperlinks of a similar level of importance. They can communicate important labeling information to the user and function as a sort of caption, neatly hidden but conveniently available. Users will feel that the material contained in this type of pop-up is useful in expanding the primary information about the hyperlink. However, users will probably not expect much depth from it because its automatic nature places the information it shows on a level similar to that of the primary information already displayed on the screen.

- *Pop-up appears when single-clicked.* When users must click on a hyperlink or hot spot to display a pop-up, they will expect the information it displays to be more important than what is shown by a rollover. This is because the user must decide that the information is likely to be useful before he or she is likely to take action to uncover it. Good interactive grammar would suggest that the writer not put trivial information in a clickable pop-up. However, in many instances the same material that would be suitable for a rollover pop-up would also be suitable for a single-click pop-up because the designer may not want to clutter the screen with rollover pop-ups and may want the pop-ups to appear only when specifically accessed. The use and impact of a single-clicked pop-up versus a rollover pop-up can be subtle, and designers may have more to say about their use than writers. Even so, writers should be aware of the distinction.

- *Pop-up appears when double-clicked.* A pop-up requiring double-clicking suggests that its information is even more important than single-click material. The fact is, however, that double-clicking has fallen out of favor and is rapidly being replaced by single-clicking. Part of the reason for this is that double-clicking can be physically tricky to accomplish; it can be particularly difficult for computer neophytes. Also, online systems don't process double-clicking well and rely almost exclusively on single-clicking. So, we might say that from a grammatical point of view, the double-click is analogous to *thee* and *thou* in English usage—it may carry a subtle difference in meaning, but it is also archaic.

- *Pop-up persistence.* Pop-ups can either stay on screen until dismissed by the user or automatically disappear when the mouse button is no longer depressed. If the pop-up stays on the screen only while the mouse button is held down, users will feel that they have more control over it. The more control users have over the display of different levels of information, the more effective the title will be. However, holding down the mouse button is part of the *drag-and-drop* process—this is another iverb, and it has a totally different use. This may have to sort itself out as interactive grammar develops, but at first glance, it would seem to add a level of confusion to the grammatical structure of interactive media. Rollovers neatly solve the entire problem: They appear when the cursor rolls over the hot spot, linger as long as the cursor is there, and go away when the cursor leaves.

Pop-up boxes form part of the writer's toolbox and will be discussed again in Chapter 13.

Navigation

Another fundamental group of iverbs are the navigational controls. These are

- Go Forward
- Go Back One Step
- Go Back to the Beginning
- History

The first three, which can be displayed as arrow icons, as words, or as both arrows and words, can be used as straightforward linear navigation tools. In this way they function in a manner generally analogous to turning to the next page, turning back to the previous page, or going back to the beginning of the book. They allow the linear exploration of interactive material.

Because interactive material is generally followed according to the intuitive path taken by each user, the middle two buttons can also be used to retrace that path one step at a time or all at once. They can work in reverse—they allow you to go back to each link that was previously followed. Because the path yet to be taken cannot, by definition, be known in advance, the forward button is useless except to retrace a previously followed path that already has been followed in reverse, or to move to the next logical step in the interactive structure. Interactive material that is more or less straightforward in its logical layout can support this function, but other material will not because there is no logical next step in the progression.

The History function is a little more complex and requires a little more skill to use. It has many implementations, but generally it presents a list of all the topics that the user has visited, either in the current session or since the title was first run. Each topic in the list can be accessed by clicking on it. This provides a way to navigate through those topics that have been previously viewed without having to go back one step at a time. However, it is possible that the list of topics may not be adequately labeled, so the user may not be given enough information to be able to use this list effectively. For example, if the user has been using hypertext to navigate through a web of ideas and wants to go back to a particular idea, it may be difficult to remember and identify it. There are better ways to create a history navigation function, but that takes creativity. In any case, navigation controls are essential, and they are fundamental in linking together inouns.

Multimedia Links

Hyperlinks that launch playback of a video, animation, or sound are fundamental to a multimedia title. They are a type of hyperlink, but they are often set off graphically so the user knows what to expect when clicking on them. This may be accomplished through some sort of iconic representation (for example, a speaker icon can be used for audio hyperlinks and a movie camera or television set icon for video), or some other graphic device may be used so that the layout tells the user what to expect. Such representation is particularly important when linking to multimedia objects in an online title; the user should be forewarned that a lengthy download time may be imminent. But it is possible to ignore any notion of advance warning and simply integrate the multimedia elements into the text in a logical fashion. Consider the following statement:

"Beethoven lived in an *apartment* at 92 Döblinger Hauptstrasse in Vienna while he composed the *Eroica Symphony*."

It is possible that when we click on the word *apartment* we would see a picture of this apartment in Vienna (restless and tormented genius that he was, Beethoven moved over 80 times during his 35-year stay in that city). In addition, when we click on the words *Eroica Symphony* we would hear a musical selection. In this case, the multimedia elements are used in a logical way, and we may need no advance tip-off that we will be hearing or seeing something. Of course, instead of playing music from the *Eroica* we could show a photograph of the autograph score, but the point is that if the logic works, then the user need not be alerted in advance.

The problem with indicating the type of multimedia element iconically or graphically is that the user may be attracted to these elements and may go through the title simply playing all the audio or viewing all the video clips. While such choices certainly are legitimate in an interactive world, it may disrupt the author's intent and deintegrate the multimedia material.

Drag and Drop

The most interactive of all the iverbs is the *drag-and-drop* function. This is accomplished by clicking on a hot spot and holding down the mouse button while moving the mouse, which moves the hot spot to another location on the screen at which point the mouse button is released. This complex set of moves is used for a wide range of interactive functions. The process is so complex that it does not fall into the hyperlinking category, but it accomplishes a very tactile and logical process that duplicates real world activities more closely than anything that could be done with a book. Consider the following example:

A screen shows a graphic representation of a living room. On the far wall is a bookcase that holds a stereo system. To its right is a rack of compact discs: You can read the label of each one. If you want to listen to any of these discs, you could click and hold the mouse button down on its label and move the mouse, thereby "dragging" the CD, so the CD covers the compact disc player in the stereo system. When you release the mouse button, an animation shows the CD loading into the CD player and the music plays. Similarly, you could drag and drop an image of a video-cassette onto a representation of a VCR, launching a video clip.

A more advanced use of drag and drop appears in Microsoft's *Encarta* multimedia encyclopedia in a demonstration of planetary forces. The screen shows an animated diagram of a satellite circling a planet, and the user is instructed (via text) to drag and drop the satellite at various distances from the planet. The program calculates the interactions between gravitational and centrifugal forces and determines whether the satellite will go hurtling out into space, hit the planet, or if the correct balance is achieved, orbit the planet.

A more fundamental use of drag and drop is the scrapbook feature used in some CD-ROM titles. The screen shows a graphic representation of a scrapbook, which is located in the same place on all screens. Any text, video, or audio throughout the title can be dragged and dropped into the scrapbook for future reference, or possibly for printing or cutting and pasting into a word processing program.

Despite the fact that it is labor intensive, drag and drop is very effective because it gives the user intimate control over action and content in a satisfying manner. Earlier in this book, we noted that the best interactive ebook titles are those that retain the best characteristics of paper books while expanding their functionality. One of the most difficult obstacles to overcome in the new media is the glass screen between the information and the user. This tends to discourage any intimate contact between the user and the ebook. But iverbs such as drag and drop give users a direct relationship between their actions and the viewed response on the screen. Using drag and drop, users can physically move information around the environment, and thus feel in control.

Buttons

Buttons are three-dimensional visual representations of the real buttons used on electronic equipment and appliances. In essence they are the same as hot spots, but they can be animated to simulate the effect of pressing down and releasing when you click on them with the mouse. Most buttons perform a specific action when clicked. Usually they offer a new set of choices, begin a process, or simply allow other choices to be processed. They can be used to signify that all of the choices made previously are to be accepted (the Okay button), or to cancel an action that has begun (the Cancel button), or they can act as ordinary hot spots.

When buttons act as hot spots, the user is given a sense that they have a high level of importance. For example, a title may have several distinct sections, and a series of buttons may allow the user to choose the desired section to visit. This type of iverb represents a high-priority action. Buttons are often used in conjunction with other iverbs, as described below.

The button has an advantage over any other control: It has a label that can define exactly what will happen when it is clicked. On the other hand, buttons usually need labels because clicking them performs actions that are otherwise undiscoverable. For instance, the button that initiates the printing process must be labeled with the word Print (or have a printer icon) or the user might not know what it does.

The most common button is simply labeled Okay because clicking on it performs the final in a series of actions. One exception to this is the Okay button that dismisses a message box that comes on the screen to alert the user to some abnormal function or to the consequence of an action. Because the computer program has no way of knowing how long the user needs to read such a message, or even if the user was looking at the screen at the time the message was displayed, such messages remain on the screen until the user dismisses them.

In most cases, the Okay button submits a series of prior user choices to the system for processing. Consider, for example, the use of a search engine. The user types the word or phrase to be searched into the search term field. When the user has completed typing the search query, there may be some other options that must be addressed, such as the selection of how broad the search should be, for example, whether to search just the current site, or whether to expand the search to the entire Web, or perhaps to limit the search by specific dates. Once these selections have been made, the user is ready to begin the search, and clicks the Okay button. In this situation, the Okay button may be labeled Start Search, but the idea is that the action is begun by clicking on the button.

Buttons are extremely important to interactive design because they bridge the gap between intangible information on the screen and the sensation of physical control. In fact, using a mouse to point to and then click a button is almost identical in feel to pressing a real button with a stick. There is only a slight dissociation from the act as it would be perceived in the real world. An excellent example of this is the use of virtual audio and video controls. Suppose you wanted to embed a link to a short audio clip into a text. When the clip is played, some graphic representation of a tape recorder control panel may be presented on the screen. This control panel has a series of buttons that mimic the controls found on a compact disc player, as shown in Figure 11.1. These controls represent play, pause, stop, reverse, and so on. Sometimes these buttons are accompanied by a slider control that users drag along its track to locate the part of the audio track they want to hear. In any case, these virtual controls have analogues in the physical world. Similar controls are also used for the display of video. Users do not need to learn how these controls function because they are based on real-world tools with which they are already familiar.

Check Boxes and Radio Buttons

Often the user is given a list from which to make selections. If the choice of items on the list is not mutually exclusive, check boxes can appear next

Figure 11.1 This is an application that controls the playing of a music CD in a computer running Windows 95. The transport controls are typical of applications that mimic real world devices.

to each item that the user can select by clicking in each box, as shown in Figure 11.2. If the selections are mutually exclusive, however, the current convention is to use small circles that fill in when they are clicked, as shown in Figure 11.3. These are called *radio buttons*, because they act like the old-style radio station buttons that mechanically forced out the old selection when a new one was pressed. These allow only one choice in a set of selections. Anyone who has ever filled out a questionnaire knows that some questions contain a list with the instructions "Check all that apply." Here we would use a check box. If the instruction read "Check only one," we would use radio buttons.

Let's assume that you are writing an interactive article for a Web site or ebook on gardening. Suppose that you have decided to provide the user with a means to select flowers for a garden. You might decide to provide selection criteria as follows:

- Seasonal: Annual or Perennial
- Color: Red, Yellow, Blue, White, Orange

The selection of annual or perennial is presented as two radio buttons, one next to the word "annual" and one next to the word "perennial." The user can select either annual or perennial but not both. But the

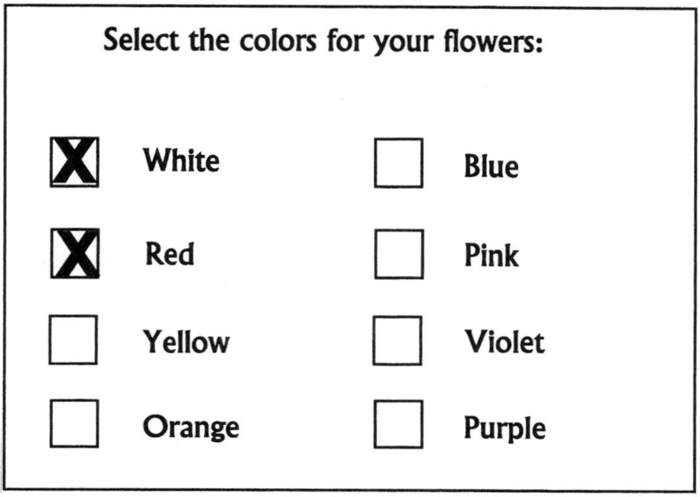

Select the colors for your flowers:
X White
Blue
X Red
Pink
Yellow
Violet
Orange
Purple

Figure 11.2 A color selection dialogue box for the selection of flower colors. By using check boxes, the user is permitted to select more than one color. As shown here, the user has selected red and white.

color selection poses a different problem—flowers can be more than one color at a time. In this case, check boxes are used. Check boxes look exactly like what they sound like, except their selection is usually indicated by a toggling on and off "*X*" inside the box. Thus, the user can select the check box next to any of the colors in our example.

Often check boxes and radio buttons are combined with type-in fields and regular buttons into groupings within a dialogue box. In this way all

Select your flower type:
Annual
Perennial

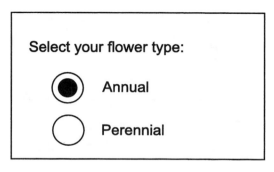

Figure 11.3 Here's how radio buttons are used to make exclusive selections. Annual *or* perennial may be selected, but not both.

of the selections can be made and information filled in before a final Okay button is clicked. This gives the user a chance to make changes before submitting the selections to the program for processing.

Dialogue Boxes

A dialogue box is often employed so the user can access desired information or perform an action that responds to his or her input. These complex iverbs are called dialogue boxes because they communicate with the user, usually in text, and the user is requested to respond by entering text into a space called a *field*, or by checking check boxes or radio buttons, as shown in Figure 11.4. This two-way communication can become more complex as the elements of the dialogue box respond to the user's input. For example, if the user selects one check box, a new set of responses may be generated that request more input. A simple dialogue

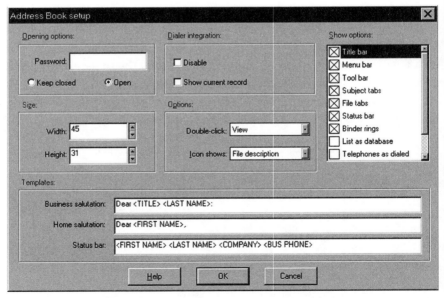

Figure 11.4 A typical dialogue box in a Windows 95 application. It has check boxes, radio buttons, and fill-in fields along with text-based communication to the user.

box is often used for searching. The user is given instructions to enter text. Next, an Okay or Begin Search button is clicked. This dismisses the box and begins the search.

Often a dialogue box contains fields to be filled in, check boxes, radio buttons, regular buttons, and tabs. Tabs are the top portions of graphical representations of file folders, which usually contain identifying labels. When a tab is clicked, that file folder moves to the front of the stack. This metaphor was introduced in Windows 3.1 and was made an official part of the Windows interface in Windows 95. It is also part of the Macintosh interface. When dialogue boxes contain many elements, we say that they become interactive sentences or *isentences*.

Whenever users must respond to a dialogue box, they must pause in the forward movement of their exploration of an interactive title. This has the effect of slowing down the action. For that reason, very complex dialogue boxes are generally used only to set up a title or program and are rarely used after that. However, users do feel that they are in control when faced with a dialogue box because the boxes are very interactive. The downside, of course, is the annoyance of having to respond.

Select

The most obvious example of the function of an iverb is the action of making a selection. Here the user performs an action on an inoun that prepares the inoun for further action. Let's assume that you find some text as a result of a search, and you want to print it out or copy it into a word processor. You might want to select the part of the text that is of interest to you. Do this by dragging the cursor over the text, which highlights it in reverse type. When you release the mouse button, the text remains highlighted because now you need the mouse to select the action you wish to take. You can select Print or Copy from a menu so that you can print the selection or paste it into your word processing program. The selection process gives the user a secondary level of control over the interactive material. The user can determine what inoun will be acted upon by the operative iverb—in this case, printing or copying.

Text and images can be selected by drawing shapes around the selection. Sometimes these shapes can be drawn while holding down the mouse button. Alternatively, a marquee selection can draw a rectangle automatically when the user drags the cursor diagonally from corner to corner. In either case, the selection is highlighted by reversing its color or differentiating it in some way. It is this iverb action that prepares the inoun (text or image) for action by a process such as printing, copying, or future manipulation by the user.

Menus: Drop Down and Pull Down

Processes and navigation tools can be selected from a hierarchy of menus. The first level is the top of the hierarchy and is the only level shown at all times. Selecting one of the menu items produces the next level of possible selections, which can be selected by clicking. Sometimes this secondary menu level produces further selections, either by cascading the menu hierarchy or by producing a dialogue box when a menu item is selected.

Menu items can be selected by a rollover—called *drop-down menus* if they normally reside at the top of the screen or *fly-out menus* if they produce choices from their right or left edges. If the mouse button must remain depressed for the menu to continue being displayed on-screen, it is called a *pull-down menu*. Drop-down menus have become more prevalent as interactive designers have begun to use less mouse clicking. These are the design rules about mouse movement and clicking:

- Never require a double-click when a single-click can accomplish the same thing.
- Never require a single-click when a rollover can accomplish the same thing.

More to Come

This discussion of the iverbs, inouns (and isentences) has focused on their impact on the user and how they fit into the grammatical structure of interactive media. Later, we shall further examine these elements from the point of view of the writer's toolbox. In other words, we shall see how the writer can use these as tools to present interactive content to the user. We shall also see how the user can use the tools provided by the writer to explore an interactive title.

Summary

Interactive media is now at a point in its development that can be compared to film in its early days. Film eventually evolved a grammar that enabled its writers and directors to develop stories, characters, themes, plots, mood, pacing, and so on. Interactive media will develop such a grammar. Already, it has sufficiently developed certain functions and rules so that it is now possible to begin delineating a fundamental grammatical structure consisting of inouns (interactive nouns)—elements such as text, pictures, video, and audio, which make up interactive media—and iverbs (interactive verbs)—the actions the user can take to link the inouns together. Just as film editing synthesizes plot and emotion from the juxtaposition of different shots, iverbs and inouns affect the user and have an impact on the synthesis of different ideas in interactive media.

The User's Grammar

Grammar is the logic of speech, even as logic is the grammar of reason.
—Richard Chevenix Trench, Irish ecclesiastic, archbishop of Dublin,
from *On the Study of Words, Lecture 1* (1858).

Unlike traditional writing, interactive writing is an inherently two-way street. The user has control over the flow of the information, but the writer has presented the information so that the user can discover it in his or her own unique way. Because the traffic is going in two directions, the user needs a way to control the flow. Thus, several fundamental tools are used to explore interactive information; the most common are point, click, double click, drag and drop, select, and type. When the user applies any of these controls, there is a grammatical impact on the information flow, and therefore a psychological impact on the user. Writers need to assess this because each will affect the information in a different way. Writers have their own grammatical tools, which are explored in the next chapter. But for now, let's look at the grammatical tools that users have at their disposal.

Point

Pointing with the mouse cursor is one of the most empowering actions interactive media can provide the user. The mere ability to read or look at a screen full of information while holding a mouse or some other pointing device in your hand enhances your level of involvement compared to simply reading text. If you have ever read a book while moving your finger over the page (as some speed-reading courses advise), you know that this act of pointing brings you closer to the material by making you feel more intimately involved with it. The mouse pointer, or cursor, is even more empowering because it provides a physical link between the content and the user.

But the act of pointing does not quite enter the realm of interactivity unless it actually produces some interactive result. We shall see in the next chapter that the writer's toolbox contains many ways to make the act of pointing more informative by producing more on-screen feedback. But the fundamental element here is that having a marker on-screen that is directly responsive to a user's hand movements establishes a much more intimate relationship with the material than other forms of interactivity can. The cursor and the mouse that controls it put the user on the other side of the glass screen. To fully appreciate the impact of controlling an on-screen pointer, let's look at an interactive system that does not use one.

Consider a type of interactive device that presents the user with choices, but allows the user access to information only by pressing numbers on a numeric keypad. For example, suppose the user is presented with a map of the United States, as shown in Figure 12.1. Each state has a number printed inside its boundaries. Suppose that if the user typed a state's code number on the keyboard, statistics about that state would appear on

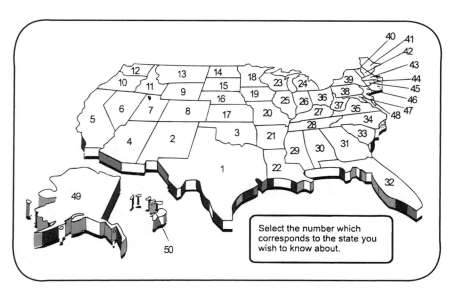

Figure 12.1 A map of the United States with a corresponding number for each state. The user can select the state by typing in the number from a keyboard or a keypad.

the screen. That would be a perfectly valid method of providing interactive control to the user, but it is indirect.

Now suppose that the user is presented with the same map of the United States, but that instead of a keypad there is an on-screen cursor that can point to each state. Note that we're not yet talking about clicking on a state, we're just talking about pointing to it. Suppose next that when the cursor enters a state's boundaries, the state's name appears in a box on the screen, as shown in Figure 12.2. By now the user is much more in control and has become more intimate with the material.

This intimacy with the material sets up a dynamic of expectations and frustration. Users feel empowered by this very basic physical relationship, but because of it they can get frustrated if the promise is not fulfilled. Users feel as if they can almost reach into the screen and pull out the information they know is there. But if they are thwarted by inefficient data organization or counterintuitive interactive design, they will feel that something is wrong. Even worse, they might wish that they had a print version that they could thumb through to find the information they need.

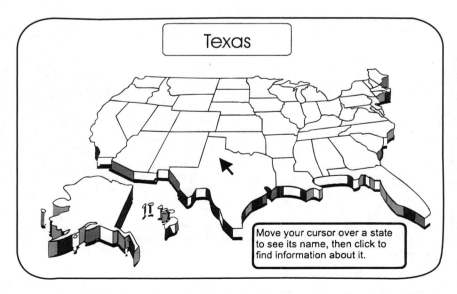

Figure 12.2 The same map of the United States but this time without the numbers. The user points to the desired state with the cursor. When the cursor enters the state's boundaries, the state's name appears in the box as shown.

The mouse cursor is the first step toward establishing user intimacy. It must be the foundation for all that follows in the interactive design of an ebook title or Web site.

Click

The mouse click is the user's ultimate control feature. If users are empowered by the ability to move the cursor around the screen, the ability to click on something completes the action. To put this into grammatical context, moving the mouse cursor is an adverb, or *iadverb*, and the click is the verb (the iverb). To make this more clear, moving and positioning the cursor modify the action of clicking, therefore, pointing modifies clicking.

Clicking is the way the user accomplishes something. If pointing produces an interactive result, such as showing the name of the state, then clicking on the state will produce a more profound result, such as displaying a box with more information about the state, hyperlinking to a different part of the content, or showing something even more interesting. During the last presidential election, there was a Web site that showed a map of the United States. At any time during the campaign until the election itself, users could use this site to help them predict the outcome of the election (or just to have fun with electoral politics). First, a user would pick the Democratic, Republican, or Reform party by pointing to an on-screen list and then clicking on the selection. As the user moved the cursor over each state, the number of that state's electoral votes was displayed at the bottom of the screen. If the user then clicked on a state, the program placed that state's electoral votes into the computer's memory and it continued to add up the votes as each state was clicked. Finally, when the magic number of 270 electoral votes (the number needed to win the election) was reached, the program displayed the chosen candidate's name and a banner that said he had won.

In this example, the act of pointing produced the information (the number of that state's electoral votes), while the act of clicking performed some action on that number (adding those electoral votes to the total). Clearly, pointing and clicking are two sides of the same coin. But they can produce different results depending on the program, and they mean different things to the user.

Double Click

Double clicking means clicking twice in rapid succession while the cursor is in the same place. This is used to signify a deeper level of importance than single clicking. But as we observed earlier, double clicking's days are numbered because focus group research has shown that most users don't like it. It is relatively difficult, and any operation the user needs to perform should be accomplished easily, without any conscious thought. We don't want the user to have to leave an intimate involvement with the material in order to consider how fast the mouse button should be clicked, or to concentrate on not moving the cursor between the clicks. Sometimes this is hard to do, so most programmers try to avoid the double click.

Another reason for the demise of double clicking is that interactive feedback on simple pointing (called rollovers) is increasingly used, and this replaces the single click. This leaves the single click available for actions that formerly required a double click. If the double click is necessary at all, it is to provide another level of importance to the click verb. To use a grammatical analogy, the double click would add an exclamation point to the single click.

Right Mouse Button Click

The mouse used for the Windows user interface has at least two buttons, unlike its Macintosh counterpart, which has only one. Since it was introduced, programmers have dabbled with ways to use the right mouse button, but Windows 95 institutionalized its use by associating it with a new element called a *context menu*. This is a floating menu that appears when the right mouse button is clicked over an item on the screen. In application programs, the context menu usually provides the ability to cut, copy, or paste (these selections are made by pointing to them and left-clicking on them). The right mouse button can have additional uses. For example, in some Web browsers, the right mouse button provides added navigation functionality.

Select

Selecting an object or text sometimes involves pointing and clicking, or it can require that the user highlight the object by pointing and holding down the mouse button while dragging across the object. In either case, the purpose is to prepare the object for a subsequent action. Selecting is effectively an interactive preposition, or *iprep*, because it places an object (an inoun) into position for action by an iverb.

Drag and Drop

Drag and drop is a complex set of user actions that provides the most intimate connection between content and the user. If point and click empowers users, drag and drop emboldens them. Drag and drop gives users the ability to physically move objects from one position on the screen to another. The objects can be words or images, and the locations can represent any object. The Macintosh originally introduced the metaphor of trashing (deleting) unwanted words or objects (files, folders, and so on) by dragging them to an iconic representation of a trash can. The user points and clicks on the object, holds down the mouse button, and drags the object by moving the mouse until the object is superimposed on the image of the trash can. The user then "drops" the object into the trash can by releasing the mouse button. Compare this with the action of pointing to an object and clicking on it to select it, then clicking on the Delete menu item or pressing the delete key on the keyboard. Clearly, drag and drop is an effective way of transferring power to the user. This action surpasses the traditional print user empowerment of page turning by allowing the user to virtually move text or objects around the page.

Drag and drop opens many creative doors for writers by allowing them to build metaphorical constructions that the user can manipulate.

For example, imagine creating a musical construction set where the screen is filled with small shapes that play sounds when they are clicked. Now imagine that the user can drag these shapes anywhere on the screen and place them in any order. The user could click on a button, which would start the sounds playing in the order in which they had been placed. In this way, the user can experiment with the construction of music.

Another example of drag and drop is the user's ability to set aside or collect pieces of information for later use. For example, if you were writing about gardening, your main content might be information about flowers and other plants. The user might want to plan a garden with selected images of flowers by dragging them to a graphic representation of a garden plot. Dragging and dropping is thus a complex verb construction that involves moving, reordering, or transforming text or objects.

Keying In

There are times when the user must provide information to the title or Web site. Sometimes this is not possible by simply selecting a list item. With a search engine, for example, the user must use a keyboard to type in the search term. In situations where it is impractical to provide a keyboard, such as in kiosks, users may be presented with an on-screen representation of a keyboard that they can use by touching in the same manner as they would a real keyboard.

Keying in information is at the top of the hierarchy of user control functions because it allows users to formulate in their own words what they want the program to respond to. Instead of manipulating information or other content provided by the writer, the act of keying in information provides users with a method of communicating to the program new information that can relate directly to the existing content. Keying in does not have the tactile response of empowerment that mouse movements have, but it works on another level that allows the most complex two-way communication between the user and the content. With mouse clicking, the user has intimate control, but only over those objects already provided on the screen. Keying in allows users to add their own objects in the form of words, numbers, or symbols on which actions can be taken, thus giving the users a different type of control over the content.

Scrolling

The electronic equivalent of page turning is scrolling in which the user reveals subsequent (or prior) sections of the screen content. Scrolling is usually accomplished by vertically dragging a slider bar on the right side of the screen down (or up to reverse the procedure) or clicking on a down- or up-pointing arrow. In some implementations, the slider has a direct relationship to content so that as the slider moves, so does the text (or other content) as if it were physically attached to some mechanism connected to the scroll bar. Other implementations show the page number change as the scroll bar is moved, but the content doesn't move until the scrolling stops once the mouse button is released.

To respond to increased use of the Web, which requires substantial scrolling, in 1996 Microsoft introduced a new pointing device called the *IntelliMouse*, which has a little wheel between the left and right buttons. When rotated with a finger, the wheel scrolls the material on the screen up or down depending on the direction in which it is turned. The wheel clicks slightly as it turns—each click corresponds to one line of text on the screen so users feel as if they are actually scrolling the content on the screen with their fingers. Additionally, the wheel can be pressed so that it locks the screen into a steady automatic scroll. The speed and the direction of the scroll can be controlled by moving the mouse up or down on the screen. The longer the distance the mouse is moved toward the top, the faster the screen scrolls upward; similarly, it scrolls down increasingly rapidly as it is moved toward the bottom of the screen.

As we shall see later in this book, the Web has virtually eliminated the page metaphor as a unit of discrete information. Because the computer monitor screen can display only so much content at a time, the use of scrolling is likely to increase.

Scrolling is only one method of revealing on-screen content. It is possible, as we have seen, to use the page metaphor and allow users to click on a representation of a page corner and "turn the page." This method brings interactive material closer to the feel of traditional paper books.

Summary

Users have many empowering tools in their toolboxes to relate directly to the content on ebook or Web site. Each tool has a greater or lesser degree of empowerment, but it is important to remember that together they provide users with a rich selection of devices with which to interact and become intimate with the content. In fact, it is this set of tools that makes the content interactive in the first place. Because these tools perform actions on the content, many of them are iverb forms or grammatical elements that constitute iverbs, iadverbs, and ipreps.

The Writer's Grammar

There is a great satisfaction in building good tools for other people to use.
—Freeman Dyson, British-born U.S. physicist

One of the distinguishing characteristics of interactive grammar is that it comes in two flavors, one for the writer and one for the user. As we observed in the previous chapter, the user's grammar consists of those actions taken by the user to direct the experience of interactive involvement with the material. Of course, the menu of actions and their consequences must be planned by the title's writer and interactive designer. This chapter explains the tools available to the writer to provide user interactivity and how the user subsequently interacts with them. This writer's toolbox is an important element in designing control and guidance into the inherently chaotic nature of interactivity.

Discoverability

One important aspect of interactive writing and design is that to be effective, the interactive elements must be discoverable. While it is possible to enclose a printed manual with a CD-ROM, or to present a page of instructions at the top of a Web home page, it is not only cumbersome but contrary to the very essence of interactive communication. If interactive media are to be as useful as traditional media, then their use must be as intuitive and free from ancillary instruction as possible. After all, when you buy a book, you don't get an instruction manual with it telling you how to turn the pages. Users must be able to navigate and discover features without prior direction or training.

Users know that they can move the mouse cursor over the page and that they can click anywhere they move the cursor. (Of course, just because they can click anywhere does not mean that the click will accomplish anything—they must click on a hot spot or hyperlink for there to be any result.) Any further required action by the user will have to be communicated from within the material itself. New features should present themselves via a simple rollover or mouse click. Thus, the new feature is said to be discoverable by the user. Once users discover a feature, they will add that feature to their vocabulary by mentally noting its existence.

Rollovers

The most intuitive and discoverable feature of any interactive title is the rollover. When the mouse is moved over a section of text or a graphic, some additional text or image appears close to the cursor that reveals additional information about the item that was "rolled over." This provides a high degree of discoverability because it requires only the most basic action on the part of the user—moving the cursor around the screen. Rollovers often provide additional details on the functionality of a feature. For example, a table of contents can be presented with a rollover that provides more detail about each chapter, or pictures can be shown with text descriptions appearing as rollovers.

Rollovers act as temporary modifiers of interactive nouns, or inouns. Thus we can call them temporary iadjectives. Thus if you were to have the sentence *The tall man hit the red ball*, you could contract it to *The man hit the ball*. The underlined words could be "hot," meaning that they would respond to the cursor when rolled over, producing a modification. Thus, when the word man is rolled over, the word *tall* would appear. And when the word ball is rolled over, the word *red* would appear. The writer provides only the necessary information in the primary sentence, but the user has the option of expanding it by rolling over the words that are shown to be hot. We see that rollovers really do act as iadjectives.

Rollovers have strong practical applications in interactive media. For example, they could be used in historical texts. Imagine writing about history and being able to leave out all but the most essential dates. Events could be described without the need to clutter the text with unnecessary date references. Historical figures could be presented with rollover modifiers showing their birth and death dates.

When you consider the implication of all of this, you see that a totally new written grammar and syntax is emerging: No longer is there a need to describe background information when writing about current or historical events. Instead, the writing can remain lean and direct. Modification and elaboration are now optional. Readers can get the gist of things yet not miss the details when they are interested. The rollover is, as previously stated, temporary. The information it reveals should therefore be short and to the point, and should not require any further action by the user.

Pop-Up Boxes

Another way to modify information is the pop-up box. The two main differences between rollovers and pop-ups are

- Pop-ups require a mouse click
- Pop-ups can remain on-screen until dismissed

Because the user must take an action that is not at first obvious, pop-ups are less discoverable than rollovers, but the information can be more lengthy and elaborate. Because the pop-up box can stay on the screen even after the mouse cursor is moved away, it can easily contain further controls such as scroll bars and action buttons. In effect, the pop-up provides more important and complex information than rollover content. Whereas a rollover is an iadjective, a pop-up box is more of a modifying phrase.

Because pop-up boxes are not easily discoverable, they should not be used where the elaborating material is very essential. In our example of historical writing, dates should be provided by either rollovers or *temporary* pop-up boxes. A temporary pop-up box remains on screen only as long as the mouse button is depressed. Once the mouse button is released, the box disappears. If there is a lot of modifying or supplemental information to be included, the temporary pop-up boxes have an advantage over rollovers in that the screen can remain uncluttered. The additional modifying information does not appear except when the user decides to click.

A good example of this application would be an encyclopedia that is cross-referenced to a dictionary. Suppose that you wanted to provide a definition for every word in the encyclopedia. It would be too unwieldy and cluttered to have a rollover definition accompany each word. Instead, it would be cleaner for the definitions to appear only when clicked upon. In this way, the user will see only selected definitions of words.

Buttons

As we observed in Chapter 11, virtual buttons are graphic representations of the real buttons we might find on an electronic device. Buttons give users the same feeling of control that they would have over an actual device in the real world. Take, for example, the action of printing something that is on a computer screen. A button might say Print just as it would if it were actually a control on the printer. This real world representation makes buttons a kind of *super iverb*. This is because the button is not actually part of the content the way a hot-linked word or hot spot on a graphic would be. Instead, it is a device involving the computer's hardware. For this reason, buttons should not be used for hot links or similar functions.

Radio Buttons

Sometimes users must make a choice from a presented list, and the choices are mutually exclusive. Only one selection can be made from the list. In this case, a special type of button called a *radio button* is used, as described in Chapter 11. Both Windows and Macintosh computers have a standardized radio button, which is nothing more than a small circle that fills with a large, solid dot when it is clicked. When one selection in the series is made, any previous choice is unselected, and that dot disappears.

Icons

Whereas one of the main benefits of buttons is their ability to contain descriptive text that tells the user what action will be taken when it is clicked, there are times when too much text makes the layout look unappealing, and perhaps slows functional comprehension. In these cases, an icon is often used. An icon is a shorthand graphic representation of an action. This action can be a function (like a button's) or it can be a hyperlink. Some icons are static; that is, they do not seem to move when they are clicked. Others either look as though they have been depressed or their colors invert when they are selected. Icons usually provide some user feedback such as changing color, adding a border, or changing the shape of the cursor to a hand with a pointing finger when they are rolled over in order to distinguish them from static background art.

Icons work because users who are exposed to them often begin to recognize them immediately. Once this is established, icons actually work better than labels because they can be recognized more quickly. This process is similar to the way international iconic symbols have become integrated into our daily routines. Originally, international symbols were meant to avoid language disparity problems. But through assimilation, people have learned to respond to them more quickly than if they had to read the actual words they represent.

Menus

A menu is a text list from which the user makes a selection. The most common of these are the menus that appear across the top of most programs. Menus usually provide a selection of functions that can be performed or links that can be followed. But sometimes menus provide navigational aids such as forward and back, or historical lists that trace the links the user has most recently followed.

Writers generally do not need to be concerned with function menus because they are part of the program rather than the content. Web browsers contain their own navigational and other menus that provide standard functions, such as the ability to print out what is on the screen. Writers of CD-ROM titles have more flexibility in menu use, but again, it is more of a programming than a content issue.

Drop-Down Fields

In some instances, the user is required to type in something to perform a function. We have already described the search function in which the user must type in the term or phrase to be searched. But often user input is limited and can be provided in the form of a drop-down menu field or list box. For example, suppose a title about music provides the user with a way to search for a favorite piece. If the field required a key-in entry, the user might type *pop* or *rock*, but the program may only have the music categorized as *pop*. So *rock* wouldn't produce any results. But if the field had a drop-down menu that listed *jazz, classical, folk,* and *pop,* then the user could not make the mistake of selecting the wrong category. An example of this type of menu is shown in Figure 13.1.

Drop-down menu fields come in many flavors. Some allow user input in addition to the choices presented, while others do not. In the former case, the menu of choices is designed to provide the user with some inspiration. In the latter, the choices are provided to force the user to choose only from those listed. This is often necessary when the input will be used as part of a database search query, where it is important that the search term is input correctly. Of course, radio buttons could be used for this function, but to use radio buttons all the selections would have to be listed on the screen. With the drop-down menu, once the selection is made the field is filled in appropriately.

Figure 13.1 A record in a database used for cataloguing compact discs. By predefining the names of the categories of music in the drop-down list shown, the user is less likely to misspell an entry, and this ensures that any search will show correct results.

Summary

The writer must provide the features the user will use to access the information and interact with it. While users have their own grammar of mouse moves, pointing, clicking, and so on, writers (or interactive designers) must determine what features are to be offered to the user as a result of their actions. Writers must think in terms of useful feedback in the form of rollovers, pop-up boxes, buttons, radio buttons, menus, drop-down fields (or list boxes), and icons. These all vary in their level of discoverability as well as their appropriateness to different functions in an interactive title.

14

Interactive Sentences: Designing the Perfect Data Chunk

I must clarify obscurities; I must make clearer definite ideas or dissociations.
—Ezra Pound

Now that we know something of the parts of interactive speech, we may ask how to best use interactive speech to express ideas effectively. Learning these fundamentals makes us more aware of the power we have, and shows us how to communicate more precisely and effectively. Like the author of a printed text, the interactive writer's primary tools are words. But not only do we use words to communicate ideas, we also use them to label sections of the content, direct the user to the correct actions, and help the user to navigate. We also use images, sound, video, animation, and interactive segments, sometimes requiring that users input their own words, which are then processed into requests for new information.

The Rules of the Interactive Road

Writers approaching interactive material for the first time, whether it is an entire CD-ROM title or a segment for a Web site, should consider the following basic rules:

- Keep it short.
- Keep it self-contained.
- Think multimedia.
- Use creative interactivity.
- Think sidebars.

- Integrate footnotes, bibliographies, and supporting material.
- Determine levels of information modification.
- Use screen metaphors carefully.

Keep It Short

Brevity is the soul of interactivity. Information is best presented in short chunks. This allows the content to be hyperorganized and it moves things along. When you drive, you tend to pay attention when you are looking for an address or when you have to make lots of turns. It is on the long stretches of highway that you tend to fall asleep. Also, as previously stated, people simply do not like to read long passages from a computer screen.

Keep It Self-Contained

The "info-chunk" must not be too dependent on what precedes and follows it. Otherwise, the interactive pathway will be restricted and the user will not move easily to or from it. Interactive writing is best when it links to many interdependent but self-contained concepts, events, characters, or ideas. For example, any large topic such as the American Civil War can be divided into battles, personalities, human rights, political agendas, economic concerns, and so on. In turn, each of these can be further divided into subsections. In this way, they can all be linked so that a character such as Robert E. Lee can be linked to many of the battles, speeches, ideas, geography, and so on.

Think Multimedia

Writers should get accustomed to the fact that ideas must be expressed in the most appropriate media. Pictures, audio, and video do not simply support ideas, they express them—in many cases, better than words. As the interactive sentence evolves, it may contain multimedia elements as well as words. Thus, an interactive sentence such as "Beethoven's *Ninth Symphony* quotes text from Schiller's poem *Ode to Joy*" may be represented with hot linked selections in the appropriate places. We must hear the *Ode to Joy* in the fourth movement of the Ninth Symphony for the sentence to fulfill its interactive potential.

This example provides us with a good opportunity to explore interactive media in relation to how different media involve the user. In his 1964 book *Understanding Media: The Extensions of Man*, Marshall McLuhan introduced the concept of hot and cool media. In McLuhan's definition, cool media, such as speech or line drawings, provide little information for the user to assess. Hot media provide enough information to complete the communication with little inference on the part of the recipient. Cool media require the user to fill in the blank areas with his or her own information to complete the communication. On the other hand, hot media, such as photographs, provide sufficient information for the user to understand fully the intent of the information provider without the need for interpretation.

Hot and cool media each have their own benefits and deficiencies. Hot media leave little room for misinterpretation because the user does not need to provide his or her own supplemental information—which might not be correct. However, hot media do not involve the user as much as cool media because they do not require a mental process to complete the communication. In McLuhan's own words: "Hot media are, therefore, low in participation, and cool media are high in participation or completion by the audience."* Interactive media allow us to have it both ways. We can present a cool medium, such as text, and infuse it with a hot medium—perhaps audio or movies—all under the user's control. This broadens the user's experience because users can interact with cool media, with a high degree of involvement, then opt to heat up the medium by selecting an audio (a hot medium) component to supplement the experience.

When we read the words "Schiller's poem Ode To Joy" we are given only the words, which may not convey the full information the writer wishes us to experience. But when we click on the words "Ode To Joy" and we hear the music, our experience becomes more complete because the hot medium fills it in.

On the other hand, multimedia should not be inserted into a title or Web site just to show it off. For example, a video clip of President

---

*Marshall McLuhan. *Understanding Media: The Extensions of Man*, Cambridge, Mass: MIT Press. © Corrine McLuhan 1964, 1994.

Kennedy's "we must go to the moon" speech is shown in many encyclopedic entries dealing with space exploration. This usage does not provide any significant illumination of the idea because seeing President Kennedy make the speech does not add anything useful to the ideas of space exploration. Instead, it just seems to alert the user to the existence of royalty-free footage.

Use Creative Interactivity

If you need to demonstrate a mathematical or scientific principle, or if you need to illustrate something that the user can actually take part in, create an interactive demonstration. If you need to show how the controls of an airplane work, give the user the stick and throttle and illustrate the relationship between speed and lift by showing the relationship between the user's actions and what happens on the screen. When properly authored, demonstrations are effective learning tools. It is easy to lecture a student on the principles of air pressure and lift, but a hands-on experiment in which a wing must be designed to provide lift will teach the principles in a uniquely effective way. This is perhaps the most powerful opportunity underlying interactive multimedia.

Think Sidebars

Writers find it easiest to transfer their traditional print media training to interactive writing when they think about sidebars to their main text. Sidebars work well with interactive media; because the spatial barriers are broken down, the new media can closely integrate the sidebar material with other ideas. Short sidebars can appear as pop-up boxes or hyperlinks within existing text. This forms a closer bond with the user than the same material does in print.

Integrate Footnotes, Bibliographies, and Supporting Material

Whenever possible, link supporting material to the main content. Explanatory material, such as glossaries and footnotes, no longer need to appear at the bottom of the page or, worse, at the end of the book. It can be fully integrated into the ebook, so that information is conveyed only when it illuminates concepts and the user requests it. If the author knows that users have access to secondary information (such as definitions, citations, and explanatory notes) while they investigate main concepts, then the writing style can become more streamlined and accessible. Chunks of supporting data can be made to appear right next to their primary content at the click of a mouse. This spatial proximity enforces the relationship and makes the supporting data more a part of the dialectic of concept. In the same way that motion pictures developed a dialectic by placing two related shots next to each other to produce a new idea, the placement of supporting, defining, or modifying information near its related word-idea creates a new concept dialectic.

Determine Levels of Information Modification

As part of the organizational process, the writer must determine the type of modifiers to use. For example, consider the sentence from Chapter 13: "The tall man hit the red ball." Now leave out the modifiers so that it reads: "The man hit the ball." How the modifiers are used is up to the writer. The writer may elect to make the words "tall" or "red" appear when the words "man" or "ball" are clicked. The writer may also choose to use rollovers to reveal these modifiers. If the modifiers appear in rollovers, they will appear next to the words they modify *automatically*. It will not be the reader's choice. The subtle differences must be understood by the writer before a style is established. This holds especially true if the writer wishes to remove dates or other frequently occurring information from the main text and put it in a modifier that is visible only through user action.

Use Screen Metaphors Carefully

One of the most controversial and often poorly used grammatical structures in interactive media is the screen metaphor. This device creates an elaborate visual environment in which information resides. The environment can be a desktop, a simple room, or a more complicated real-life structure. The entire title may be presented through one of these metaphors. Within the environment are objects that can be manipulated by the user to navigate and to produce data. The problem is that if the environment is too complex, it can be cluttered, and more difficult to navigate than the real environment it represents.

A classic example of this is the museum metaphor. Because in the real world the concept of a museum is intimately linked with its content, interactive designers have frequently used (and overused) the museum as a metaphor. Thus, in a title about art, or history, or any subject where a museum is appropriate to the content, the visual environment represents an actual museum. The museum metaphor functions both as the visual receptacle in which the artifacts are presented and as its navigational mechanism. The title may open with a full screen representation of the main hall of a particular or hypothetical museum. The main information may be represented by an information kiosk, or there may be a card catalog, or signs pointing to other parts of the museum that represent specific subject areas.

For example, we might have an art museum. Signs in the main lobby could point us to the left to view the Impressionist collection or up the stairs to look at Renaissance paintings. Interspersed might be representations of the museum walls where the art is hung. Within a room there might be three-dimensional objects, such as statues or other sculpture; users may view these pieces in 360 degrees using some sort of virtual reality navigation system built into the software.

In a natural history museum, there might be a hall of mammals or of dinosaurs. There may be many graphically represented playback devices that provide audio and video clips when the user presses the controls.

Screen metaphors demonstrate a unique feature of interactive media in their ability to depart from the constricting format of print (although we've seen some metaphors that represent a real book on the screen). Often this technique is effective, but more often it is not. Screen metaphors must be carefully designed. They must provide streamlined and intuitive access to the data without clutter or distraction. They must make navigation easier than in a book or other traditional media.

Unfortunately most do not and here's why: The screen metaphor superimposes another layer of information over the primary subject matter of a title. This new layer consists of the physical layout of the environment, its idiosyncrasies, and its visual representation. This is extraneous baggage added to the direct exploration of the information. It may seem visually appealing, but it often works counter to direct intuitive access to the information.

Designers of many of the first screen metaphors that utilized the museum format did not realize that when users choose to explore the title, they are more interested in its informational content than in the experience of exploring the museum layout. Put another way, when you visit a museum you want to spend as much time as possible viewing its content and learning about it, rather than navigating its floor plan. In other words, although a realistic virtual environment may be attractive, and in some cases it may help to create a mood, it must be carefully designed so that it does not impose obstacles to access. The exception is a game title, where the environment may be an integral part of the story, and in any event wandering around and getting lost is part of the fun.

Used skillfully, screen metaphors can enhance the enjoyment of a title and provide streamlined access to the data. But to accomplish this, designers and writers need to spend the time necessary to fully analyze the relationship of the metaphor to the data and determine whether it works to the benefit of the user.

Summary

Writers need to understand basic rules of the road when creating an interactive title:

- *Keep it short.* Create small chunks of information.
- *Keep it self-contained.* Keep these chunks interrelated but not overly dependent on preceding or following information.
- *Think multimedia.* Use multimedia elements as you would words, and use the particular media best suited to the content.
- *Use creative interactivity.* Allow users to participate by providing interactive exercises.
- *Think sidebars.* Integrate sidebars into the material, and remember that electronic media do a far better job of integrating supporting and tangentially related ideas than traditional print media.

- *Integrate footnotes, bibliographies, and supporting material.* Enhancing information placed in close proximity, but doing it unobtrusively, creates tight combinations that often produce new meanings.
- *Determine levels of information modification.* Plan ahead to determine the information that will be left out of the primary level. Decide upon the method by which supporting information will be displayed.
- *Use screen metaphors carefully.* Screen metaphors provide an interesting method of structuring a title that departs from the constricting format of a paper book or other traditional media, but they must be used with extreme care because they often adversely affect information access and navigation.

15

Understanding How Interactivity Affects User Comprehension and Retention

One may say the eternal mystery of the world is its comprehensibility.
—Albert Einstein

In a printed book, it is possible to present information in such a way as to build upon previous information. In interactive media, the user controls the order in which information is received. Retention is greater when information arrives only when the user has requested it and when the user's level of interest is highest. The writer must fully understand this because user comprehension is affected by assumptions made by the writer.

Now That You Ask

If you take a classroom full of students studying geography and start feeding them data (such as the amount of bauxite Brazil produces each year), not only will their eyes glaze over, but it is likely that they will not retain much of it. If you put together an interactive title that allows the students to interact with the same material, pointing to different countries, clicking on items like agriculture, main industries, and population, they will retain much more. Why is this?

Information is retained far better when it is directed to a receptive user. The students in the first example are expected to retain information simply because they are told to. In addition, there is no synchronicity between the transmission of the information and the user's receptivity. Even when motivated enough to read a book to learn about something, the user's attention may flag; even if it doesn't, the information may not arrive when the reader's interest in that particular topic is at its highest. All linearly presented information has this problem. At best, the reader can skip around, but most linear presentations are not written to support this.

If users are able to formulate questions and request information, their level of receptivity is higher. This is exactly what happens with interactive material. Every time users move the mouse cursor and click on something, they are requesting information. Because they made the request, they want to know the information, at least to some extent. Therefore, they will retain it longer.

The corollary to this idea is that the more actively users want to interact with information, the better their retention. Thus, information provided via a rollover is less likely to be retained than information that requires a mouse click (as with a pop-up box). This should not be construed as a negative view of rollovers. Here we're talking only about the user's retention of the information, not his or her comprehension.

A high level of retention, however, should not be the only goal of interactive writers. With some content it may be more important to provide context than facts to be memorized. If a historical title places all dates associated with the events in rollovers (as we discussed in Chapter 13), the dates help place events in context and will allow the information to flow more freely than if the dates cluttered it. These dates won't be retained as well as they would be if they were presented through a pop-up box, but in this particular title that may not be as important as establishing context.

But here's the dilemma: If the dates are presented in pop-up boxes, the user might not choose to check every date because the commitment necessary to click on a hyperlink is greater than the level of effort necessary to move the mouse over a rollover. Therefore, the user might not bother. In other words, although retention may be improved when the user is involved in the title, a demand for involvement can also act as a barrier to the information.

A Matter of Levels

As we have seen, there are three main levels of interactive information:

- First Level. The highest level is that which presents the information on the screen directly. This information appears on each screen, from the first to appear to each hyperlinked screen that branches out from it.

- Second Level. The second level represents information that appears nearly effortlessly, as the mouse cursor moves over (but does not click on) the hot areas of the screen.
- Third Level. The third level contains all information that can be seen only if the user makes a conscious decision to look at it and then takes an action, such as clicking the mouse, to reveal it.

The writer must determine the appropriate levels of information and decide how they are to be organized, because the levels used affect the following important aspects of an interactive title:

- The flow of the information. The information flow can be made more streamlined if certain types of subordinate information are put into a lower level and brought forward interactively by the user as requested (such as dates in a historical title).
- The organization of information. The writer may want to focus on certain aspects of the information, such as events or personalities. Thus, an historical title might feature the personalities of the era, and so the dates and events would recede to the second and third levels. Alternatively, the title could focus on the events and put the personalities in the second or third levels. Finally (but by no means exhaustively) the title could focus on the dates and set out a chronological layout of the information, relegating both personalities and events to second and third levels.
- The need for user retention. As we've discussed, the top levels have the lowest potential for user retention of the information because the user does not need to make a conscious decision to receive it. This information appears on the screen without the user having to choose to see it. This is comparable to the level of retention you would find with a traditional linear book. But user retention should never be the writer's primary motivating principle, unless the task is writing an instructional or training title that must produce extraordinary retention levels. In those titles, the writer probably will provide interactive quizzes and other means of testing to reinforce and measure retention and comprehension.

Field Day for Control Freaks

Another reason users of interactive media show better retention than readers of linear material is that they remain in control at all times. If interest in one area of the subject wanes, the user need only to click on something else, which may be more interesting to them at the moment. The user manipulates the data so that what is most interesting at the time will always be front and center.

With traditional linear material, information flows according to the writer's plan. With interactive media, the information flows according to the wishes (and whims) of the user. This is a powerful notion. Because it is the user who is receiving the information, it is the user who most rightfully needs to control its flow, a control that linear media provide only on a superficial basis. When users have access to all of the information at one time and know that they can select any pathway into it, the experience becomes more organic. In fact, a well-designed interactive title will perfectly match its content with the user's interest and expected level of receptivity to it. Even if two different users interact in totally different ways with an interactive title, if they both explored everything in it they would both end up with an intimate familiarity with all of the material presented by the writer, each one based on his or her level of interest at the time the information arrived. So even though each one explored the material in a different order, all of the material would be absorbed, comprehended, and retained on a higher level than if it had been read straight through from a linear source.

Summary

Interactivity can affect user comprehension and retention in a very positive way. By presenting different types of information on different levels, the writer can affect the level of retention, flow, comprehension, and organization of the material. The more the user has to consciously seek the information, the better the retention.

Part Four

Interactive Storytelling

16

Computer versus Television

Television's perfect. You turn a few knobs, a few of those mechanical adjustments at which the higher apes are so proficient, and lean back and drain your mind of all thought. . . . You don't have to concentrate. You don't have to react. You don't have to remember. You don't miss your brain because you don't need it.

—Raymond Chandler

The Venue Is the Message

When Thomas Edison invented the kinetoscope, the precursor to motion pictures, he didn't intend for it to be viewed by people in large groups in the public places that today we call movie theaters. Instead, he thought that the technology would be the perfect complement to another invention of his: the phonograph. Edison thought that moving images would make the experience of recorded sound more complete. He proposed that individuals or small groups would watch the singers and musicians as they performed recorded music. It wasn't until others helped shape the theatrical film we know today that it became a group experience in which people gathered in public to watch and listen.

But the venue does have an impact. Consider TV sitcoms, for example. In television's early days, producers realized that people react differently to comedy when they see it at home by themselves than they do when they are in a theater as part of a large audience. The producers theorized that people had to be prodded into laughing when they were alone because they no longer had the socially accepted group dynamic to give them permission to laugh. Besides, people felt that only lunatics laughed by themselves. Hence, the laugh track was born—a technician with a tape of prerecorded laughter simply adds hilarity during the show's postproduction. Alternatively, when a live television show is taped before an audience, applause signs are placed throughout the studio and flashed at critical times during the show. Whatever its original purpose, you might argue that the TV laugh track is just an excuse to get people to laugh when the material isn't funny. Ethics aside, TV laugh tracks have became a staple of television comedy. It is apparently necessary because solitary viewing imposes a state of mind that is quite different from viewing in a large group. TV shows have laugh tracks, but theatrical films certainly do not. Similarly, some consideration should be given to the fact that interactive content may function differently when viewed from fourteen feet as opposed to fourteen inches from the screen.

The pejorative (but affectionate) term "couch potato" implies a passive viewer. The widely held notion behind the term is that the television viewer does not want to participate in the activity on the screen. In fact, the very use of that quasi-interactive remote control is simply to change the source of the linear content when the passive viewer is bored or otherwise uninterested in the content.

Today interactive media is in a transition period, as film was in Edison's day. Today we interact with electronic media mostly through computers. But that could (and probably will) change as computer technology infuses other devices. Computers are becoming more TV-like, and TVs are becoming more computer-like. The changes in venue change the nature of the interaction and affects the content with which viewers and users interact.

The average computer user sits roughly fourteen inches from the computer screen. This distance is within arm's length. Although the computer user interacts with the medium via a mouse or some other peripheral device, there is a sense that the screen is within reach and that the user can influence the content through intimate involvement. We once had a similar relationship to television, when we had to physically turn a knob to switch channels. But those were the days of fewer channels and before remote controls.

The TV remote is a device that has had a major effect on the medium of television. It allows the user to control the content of the medium. Of course, the control is limited to selecting channels, controlling volume, adjusting picture quality, and turning the set on and off, but the remote changed TV to such an extent that advertisers have yet to figure out how to make viewers watch and listen to their commercials.

But doesn't the existence of remote controls make television an interactive medium? Certainly not to any significant degree. The user can change the nature of the linear content by switching to another channel (with different linear content), by eliminating the audio, or by turning it all off. But the television viewer does not have the ability to interact with (and therefore dynamically change), the linear content of television. In other words, as powerful as the TV remote is, today it allows only the weakest kind of interactivity.

As computer and television technologies begin to merge, the ability to interact dynamically with the content of TV becomes technically more feasible. But the issue has become whether there is something fundamental in the experience of the television viewer that is different from the experience of the computer user. There! Look at that last sentence. Notice that when we referred to the participant in the television experience we said "viewer," but when we referred to the computer counterpart we said "user." So the question is: Does the TV viewer want to become a TV user?

The answer to that question lies in the nature of the medium, not the hardware. In short, if the television set is interactive, then we are not using it to watch television. Rather, we are doing something else. This is the same fundamental change we go through when we use the television set to view videotapes, or to watch cable movies without commercials, or to use a Nintendo or Playstation, or to watch a home video, or play a laser disc via television. The box is the same, but the medium is different.

Web TV and CD-ROM TV

As the World Wide Web becomes more popular, many of its proponents see the television set as a possible terminal from which to view the Web's content. Already, set-top boxes have begun appearing that give television viewers the ability to see Web pages on their television sets. But the way the Web works on a TV set can be very different from the way it works on a computer. If the set-top boxes don't offer a certain amount of computing power to process some of the more advanced pages that contain miniprograms called *applets*, or if they don't have some type of storage device such as a hard drive to store downloaded material, then they will offer only a very limited experience with the Web. Of course, such limited experience may be just fine for casual users.

An early version of CD-ROM called *CD-i* (Compact Disc-interactive) was promoted in the mid-1980s, primarily by Philips, as the interactive multimedia successor to the audio compact disc. It was designed to play through a set-top box for viewing, and it was operated via an infrared remote control that featured a thumb-operated joystick that moved an on-screen cursor. The software available consisted of games, children's activity programs, encyclopedias, museum tours, and movies. The system was very easy to use, and the hardware was no more difficult to hook up than a VCR. No computer knowledge was required. Yet, just as CD-ROMs for the computer were becoming successful, CD-i was unable to make any inroads into the consumer market.

What was it about CD-i that made it fail as a television-based medium? There are so many factors involved that it is very difficult to say for sure which single one was most responsible. It could be that the software was inadequate, or that the hardware was not powerful enough for it to deliver adequate performance, or it could be that it was just a victim of bad timing or bad marketing. Whatever the reason for CD-i's nonsuccess, it is an example of a television set device that failed while the same sort of content became a hit on the computer screen. Therefore, one possible explanation is that what works on a computer screen doesn't necessarily work on a television.

Summary

Edison soon caught on to the fact that people wanted to see movies in theaters, and his notion of a movie as a visual complement to music had to wait 80 years until MTV came along. Today, writers must be able to understand the dynamics between the medium and the venue. The playback venue itself affects the experience the user is likely to want. If interactive fiction, in a theatrical sense, is to work, the writer must successfully transplant the medium from the computer to the television screen. This means that the writer must understand that the *viewer* must become a *user*, and that means overcoming the inertia of passive viewing and turning watching into active participation.

17

Story Branching

Nobody has any conscience about adding to the improbabilities of a marvelous tale.
—Nathaniel Hawthorne

Choose Your Own Adventure

In the early 1970s an attorney named Edward Packard began telling interactive bedtime stories to his daughters—in these tales he let the children choose the plots. Packard decided to write down his stories so that he could share them with others. Eventually, his device of telling stories with branching plots based on the reader's choices became the enormously successful children's book series *Choose Your Own Adventure*.* What is truly remarkable about Packard's success is that his stories were published in ordinary paperbound books with nary a computer in sight.

Packard used the device of printing the various plot elements in nonlinear form. At the end of each section, where a choice must be made, the reader is instructed to turn to a specific page based on that choice. So a typical story might have the following menu at the end of a section:

If you decide to explore the cave opening to the right, turn to page 33.
If you decide to swim across the river, turn to page 84.
If you choose to build a campfire and wait until a rescue team arrives,
turn to page 91.

---

*Packard joined with R. A. Montgomery to write the *Choose Your Own Adventure* book series. Although they each wrote many of the books, they also employed other writers to author books in the series.

Once the reader turns to the appropriate page, the story progresses until another set of choices is offered. The reader selects choices that ultimately lead to the end of the story. Sometimes this ending choice can occur early on in the plot. Other times the story goes on at length, with many plot twists and turns.

Packard's work ranks among the most successful of all children's book series. And all of this was done without computer technology. But perhaps that is the very reason for his success. Without the need to show off technology, Packard was able to concentrate on the essence of interactive storytelling. The story itself was the focus, not the hardware.

Interactivity and Free Will

At the heart of Packard's storytelling system is the nearly organic integration of device and plot. The choices are always comparable to the real life choices we all make. In real life we are constantly presented with choices. Should I make a right or a left turn here? Should I have a ham sandwich or sushi? Should I be an investment banker or an artist? All of these options represent doors through which we can travel. Open one and the others usually close. Choices represent a fundamental aspect of our humanity because they are the expression of our free will. Because traditional literature does not offer an effective way of expressing our free will, interactive media may be the best way to explore this very human property.

Interactivity Should Not Be a Crutch

Of course, interactive media are not only for philosophical exploration. They are for entertainment as well, and it is through entertainment that most writers seek to express themselves. To be truly entertaining, stories must succeed on their own. In short, a writer who uses interactivity as a crutch for poor writing is destined to fail.

Writers need to develop entertaining stories with the following elements:

- Strong characters
- Inventive plotting

- Interesting settings
- Powerful emotional content
- Provocative themes

The presence or absence of any of these will strongly influence the success or failure of an interactive title, just as they would a traditional linear one.

Unreality and Natural Choices

The most successful interactive ebook titles (or Web sites, or interactive television) feature choices that flow from the story and the characters. To abruptly stop the action for the purpose of requiring the user to make a choice pulls the user out of intimate involvement with the material that good writing provides, and splashes cold water on the reader's suspension of disbelief. This suspension of disbelief is achieved when good writing brings the reader into direct contact with the material to the exclusion of the outside world. When reading good material, the reader is often unaware of the surroundings as the mind builds pictures of the images the writer has conjured. Readers of well-written fiction are often unaware of turning the pages or the sounds of the real world environment by which they are surrounded while reading the book. But if the reader is jarred by the need to make choices then the flow of the book is interrupted, and the reader probably will not develop intimate contact with the material.

The way to avoid this is to make sure that the required choices are natural and flow from the story itself. For example, if the story puts the protagonist in peril and requires a choice of an exit route, the story must bring users to the point where they would naturally be making such a choice even if the medium were not interactive. The *Choose Your Own Adventure* series accomplishes exactly this, and is therefore successful in integrating interaction with a state of unreality.

Offering the Reader Several Choices

One difference between interactive fiction and the real world is that in the real world the user has a theoretically infinite number of choices. In interactive fiction, the writer must provide these choices for the user, because the mechanics of plotting require that the writer maintain control over the branching.

Of course, from a technological standpoint the writer could allow infinite choice, but the user would then be able to follow pathways that eventually would make no sense. This would be like providing the user with a piano (and, of course, the freedom to hit any key in any order) but no instruction on playing it. The user's ability to create decent music would depend entirely on his or her skill, and an untrained user would produce discordant noise. Similarly, offering users infinite choices would be akin to offering them a word processor. Only a skilled writer would come up with anything remotely satisfying.

Therein lies one of the pitfalls of interactive writing. The writer must overcome the desire of most readers to enjoy a well-plotted narrative. When such works are successful, they plot out in only one direction and lead inexorably to a single possible ending. User intervention in most cases will provide inferior storytelling unless the writer is skilled and takes care to make the choices natural and evocative of free will.

Multiple Beginnings, Middles, and Endings

The simplest interactive fiction offers several beginnings, middles, and endings. Typically these will offer the user several paths, limited to the main areas of development.

- *Beginnings*. The writer creates several sets of exposition that establish the setting and characters, set the tone, and launch the plot. Any choice made by the user must dovetail with the middle and ending choices.
- *Middles*. The development of the story, including plot twists, must work with any of the previously selected beginnings and all of the yet-to-be selected endings.
- *Endings*. The endings must take any of the possible combinations of beginnings and middles to a satisfactory conclusion.

Clearly, the use of multiple beginnings, middles, and endings can constrain the user and often has the effect of turning the story into a game rather than a satisfying narrative. To overcome this, the writer must add a level of complexity so that the story is much more fluid. To achieve this, the writer may choose not to use multiple beginnings. This makes it easier to establish a plot, characters, and setting that can flow into any combination of subsequent plot turns.

It is most effective to retain multiple endings, so that the story can be experienced many times without the user knowing how it will end up. This tends not to work with riddles and mysteries, however, because they generally have only one satisfying ending.

Plot Complexity and Chaos Theory

The writer may need to develop a degree of choice complexity that works on many levels and may turn the plot on itself depending upon the user's choices. To develop complex interactive plots the writer might want to become a student of chaos theory, which uses the analogy of the butterfly effect. In this metaphor, chaos theory is demonstrated by noting that a butterfly beating its wings in one part of the world will create a disturbance that ultimately will have an effect on weather patterns throughout the world. Tiny eddies coming off the butterfly's wings affect larger and larger patterns of moving air, so that a tornado in another hemisphere might be explained by such a minor event.

In terms of plot, let's consider the case of a car accident: A businessman is driving a car and listening to the news on the radio when he hears that a conglomerate has announced a hostile takeover of his firm. Simultaneously, a girl on rollerblades shoots out in front of the car just as the driver glances at the radio's volume knob to turn it up so he can catch the details about the takeover. He doesn't see the rollerblader until the last minute, and he swerves to avoid her. The driver misses the skater, but hits a garbage can that rolls into the street just in time to throw a bicyclist off course and into a ditch.

In this example there are many plot points that account for the outcome. If any of these plot points were different, the outcome would have been different.

- If the businessman worked for a different company, the news item on the radio wouldn't have caught his interest and he would have been paying attention to his driving.
- If the investment banker who orchestrated the takeover that was announced on the radio had missed his plane and so had not been able to consummate the deal, there would have been no story to distract the driver.
- If the businessman had picked up his son earlier, the radio might have been tuned to a different station and the news story would not have distracted him.
- If the rollerblader had not had her Walkman headphones on earlier, she would have heard the phone call from her friend and would have gone to the mall with him instead of going skating.

You get the idea. This level of complexity demonstrates the principle of chaos theory applied to plot complexity. Even with a relatively small number of choices, a tremendous number of plot possibilities are generated.

Summary

As a practical matter, the writer must be disciplined enough to maintain satisfying plot branches and keep track of all of the permutations. No matter how complex the interactive plot choices become, the writer must adhere to the same rules that make any noninteractive title work well. Choices work best when they represent the natural choices of real life. In this way, they won't jar the reader and interrupt the flow of the story.

18

Involving the Reader/User: Using the Second Person

You walk into the room with your pencil in your hand. . . .
—Bob Dylan (from "Ballad of a Thin Man")

Second Person Interactive

As with other languages, the English language identifies three different points of view. Each is called a *person* and refers to one of three possible subjects: the person speaking (first person), the person spoken to (second person), and anyone or anything else (third person). Each has a singular and plural form; respectively, they are I/we, you/you, and he, she, it/they. (The second person is unique in that it does not distinguish between singular and plural forms.) A first person singular sentence might read, "I see a strange-looking man." Second person singular might read, "You see a strange-looking man." And third person singular might read, "She sees a strange-looking man."

The third person is as much at home in interactive fiction as in traditional linear fiction. If the subject is "he" or "the man" we have no trouble following that character throughout the story, and we have no trouble manipulating what that character says and does. But the third person offers little dynamic involvement for the user because it puts the user outside the story that is about a "he," "she," or "it." The first person is almost never used in interactive fiction because users have difficulty manipulating the protagonist if it is "I"; if a story is told from that point of view users will have difficulty telling the storyteller what happens to him. If the story begins with "I followed the strange-looking man down the tunnel," how can the user tell the storyteller "No, you did not follow the man down the tunnel; you waited for him to emerge from the doorway."

Interactive fiction often uses the second person to tell a story. In this chapter we'll cover some of the issues and difficulties writers may encounter using what we will call the second person interactive.

Who's on Second?

Interactive fiction requires much more user involvement than traditional fiction because the user is asked to participate in the story. In essence, the writer is asking for help in writing the story; because the user isn't getting paid for it, there had better be other compensation to induce participation. One of the most effective ways of getting the user involved is to make him or her the protagonist. If the user is the protagonist, then the user will have the motivation to make the choices required to move the plot along. When writers use the second person in interactive fiction, we say they are using the second person interactive.

Most interactive stories in the second person begin with something like this:

> You see a strange-looking man scurry down a dark alley and climb up a fire escape. You notice that he is carrying a large package.

In this way the story unfolds through the eyes of the user. All other characters may or may not take actions, but the writer must first decide what level of interactivity the user will be allowed. In our example, the user, who just saw a man scurry down the alley and up the fire escape, might have to decide what action to take.

However, the writer may decide to allow different scenarios. Three men might scurry down the alley, or the strange-looking man might not scurry, but instead steal something and climb through a first floor window. The point is that the writer can choose to have many different levels of interactivity while the user remains the protagonist. Using our example, here are just a few possibilities for user interaction:

- You see a man scurrying down an alley and you decide to follow him.
- You see a man scurrying down an alley and you decide to call the police.

- You see three men scurrying down an alley dragging what seems to be a body inside a duffel bag. You decide to follow and investigate.
- You see three men scurrying down an alley dragging what seems to be a body inside a duffel bag. You decide to scream for help.

In these examples, the user has the choice of taking one or more actions and the action has two variants (one man or three, scurrying or dragging a duffel bag). The level of interactivity is indicated by the possible user intervention against several possible external scenarios.

Problems with the Second Person

Writers of interactive fiction will find that while you have many opportunities to develop a plot using the second person, the level of internal discourse is severely limited. If "you" are the protagonist, the writer cannot impart a character history or background story to you or discuss your emotions. In short, the main character must remain superficial. Of course, it is possible for the writer to impart emotions, motivations, and backgrounds to other characters, but a device must be found that will allow the writer to communicate these to the user who is the protagonist. So it might be possible for the protagonist to find a diary and read about how the strange-looking man in our example came to be scurrying down the alley, what he was trying to accomplish, and why. For example, the narrative might go like this:

> You follow the strange-looking man scurrying down the alley. You notice that he has dropped something and you decide to wait until he has gone through one of the doors into the building so you can pick it up without being seen. You see he has dropped an envelope. You open it and read: "Your son has not been harmed. You will find him in the basement of 552 Riverview Drive at midnight. Make sure you bring $1 million in small-denomination unmarked bills."

If the characters interact directly with the user that interaction must be plot-driven, because the characters cannot be made to know the user's nature or personality. They can know what actions the user has taken within the confines of the story, but little else. So it is possible for the man scurrying down the alley in our example to notice the user and confront him. This would require that the user choose how to respond, but this is more plot- than personality-based. For example, the strange man might say to the user, "Why are you following me?" And the user might have the option of running away or answering with such prewritten answers as "I want to know what you are doing." But this dialogue must be prewritten, and the user cannot truly feel in control. Of course, it would be far more difficult to write an interactive story about a relationship involving the user, because the writer cannot write the user's character.

It is possible to create a character for the user to choose at the outset, or even to create a single character that the user must assume ("You are the commander of a World War II submarine on a secret mission. . . ."), but this approach is limited when compared to traditional writing. It would be very difficult to write a love story or a psychological thriller in the second person interactive, even when a character or a personality is assigned to the user, because an internal monologue is difficult to convey in the second person.

Difficult, yes, but not impossible. In fact, this is where interactive fiction puts great demands on the creativity of the writer. Here are a few story challenges and some solutions.

A Psychological Thriller

The problem posed by a psychological thriller is how to communicate the inner workings of the mind of the antagonist when the story is written in the second person. If the user is the protagonist, then he or she must stop an action—perhaps a murder or a bomb blast—from happening, or solve a mystery. One way to do this is to have the antagonist write letters or diary entries. Perhaps one of the characters might be a psychiatrist who can reveal the antagonist's inner working. When the user-protagonist interacts with the antagonist, the computer program can keep track of these events and generate different psychological states for the antagonist, and these states can be revealed in any of the methods mentioned.

A Love Story

Interactive love or relationship stories using the second person are difficult to write because by definition they must reveal the protagonist's inner thoughts and emotions. Because the protagonist is the user, he or she cannot be placed in an unwelcome emotional state. In traditional writing, the reader arrives at an emotional state through the skill of the writer; the writer achieves the intended result by describing the characters' emotions and putting them in emotion-evoking situations. Interactive fiction cannot effectively ask the user to feel a certain way. The writer could say, "You feel threatened and helpless . . ." but that may or may not reflect the reality of the user's emotional state and in any case obviously is very limp writing.

Love stories can be successful if they abandon the second person in favor of the multiple third person narrative and present the story through the eyes of one character at a time. The story can become properly complex because it can offer the user the opportunity to live the story through any character and switch characters at will throughout the story. Add to this plot choices, and the interactivity can get nicely complicated as the user switches points of view and makes plot choices simultaneously.

The Ultimate Interactive Fiction

Interactive fiction opens up many opportunities for all types of writers. The ability to explore the elements of reality or fantasy through multiple plot pathways and simultaneous multiple points of view, and to revisit situations through the eyes of other characters, is a rich and highly creative way to write. Although writers who attempt will be menaced by many, many pitfalls, it is an exciting new challenge for them.

Here's an example of the kind of opportunity offered writers of interactive fiction to explore subject matter as theoretical as the nature of reality:

Suppose we operate on the premise that our perceptions of reality all come to us through our senses. Everything we know about the world arrives through nerve pathways from our eyes, and ears, and our senses of touch, smell, and taste. Now suppose that we posit the notion that our consciousness is nothing more than a plasma of energy in a jar in a laboratory in some far-off spot in the universe, and that it is being electronically fed everything we experience. This book you are reading, the existence of everyone and everything you know, is simply the result of an electrical current fed into that consciousness.

You might say "But that's impossible. If that were true, how would people and events react to my actions? How could I affect anything if everything I experience was simply being fed into my consciousness?"

The answer, of course, is the ultimate interactive computer. If everything you experienced was the result of digital information generated by a computer and fed directly to your brain in response to your thoughts, then a computer somewhere might be analyzing your thoughts and returning new data directly to your consciousness in dynamic response.

This is an example of where things might be headed. From a technological standpoint everything described above is theoretically possible (except perhaps for your disembodied consciousness sitting in a jar in some laboratory). If we connect our computer to a virtual reality generator that feeds back visual images and realistic audio, and have it all respond to our decrypted brain waves, then such a fantasy might be possible. In such a case, the second person interactive would enter the real world. Or would it? How would we know?

Summary

Interactive fiction can use any of the three points of view: The first person (I, we), the second person (you), or the third person (he, she, it, they). The first person is rarely used because it is difficult for the user to manipulate the storyteller if "I" am telling the story. The third person can be used, but it offers no dynamic involvement for the user, because the user is an outside observer of a story involving "he," "she," "it," or "they."

The point of view used most often for interactive fiction is the second person—what we call in this context the second person interactive. This point of view offers nearly unlimited opportunities for writers of interactive fiction because it places users at the heart of the action and puts them in complete control. The only limitations are in the areas of internal discourse where users cannot be made to feel or think things that real-life users aren't thinking or feeling at the time they are interacting with the material.

Technology can provide virtual reality experiences in the second person interactive that come very close to the real world and possibly even surpass it, at least in some creative sense.

19

Being Creative: Enriching the Title

True creativity often starts where language ends.

—Arthur Koestler

At this point in the book we would like to explore a tangent and assess the underpinnings of structure in order to create a groundwork for future experimentation. At first glance the motive may appear ill-conceived because any preconceived notions of structure potentially can limit creativity. We must say to our readers that we hope this isn't so. Particularly in the area of fiction, the rulebook has yet to be written. We can only guess where we are going. We think that any structural bounds are weak under the force of creative urges. In other words, rules don't rule.

In this chapter we will discuss some ideas for interactive fiction that can add to our concepts of interactive plotting and viewpoint. But bear in mind that under no circumstances should this be construed to be part of any exhaustive plan or structure. These are some ideas to get your creative juices flowing and to suggest to you some of the ways that new technology can liberate rather than constrain writers.

See the Book, Read the Movie

Hitherto, we have discussed interactive fiction as if it were solely an extension of the paper book. Of course, that may be a logical starting point, because whatever the medium, it all begins with the written word. Even movies start from paper scripts. But the new media offer writers many ways to communicate with the user. Here are the principal ways interactive media are currently used in fiction:

- *Interactive novels.* This category is the interactive extension of the traditional book. The user reads and follows the story until asked to make a choice by the writer.
- *Interactive movies.* These are extensions of narrative movies. They can begin simply as a linear branching narrative, with the plot essentially moving forward but taking different paths based on user choices. Alternatively, the story can turn back on itself creatively, reusing plot elements.
- *Hybrids.* The plot may begin with the user reading some opening text, and then perhaps seeing a video introducing some plot elements or characters. The plot can be advanced using any media, including text, audio, animation, virtual reality, gamelike elements (perhaps the user can shoot some bad guys), or even filmed footage.
- *Nonnarrative stories.* These often fall into the category of games, but they are really stories in which users find themselves placed into a preexisting situation and/or environment and required to solve some sort of puzzle, such as a murder mystery, to escape from the environment, or to find the meaning of life. The CD-ROM game *Myst* is prime example of this type of nonnarrative story.

Interactive Novels

Interactive novels may be the easiest form for writers who wish to experiment with the new media. The narrative can be developed in short segments and easily flow-charted. Of course, interactive novels can get very complex, as discussed in Chapter 17. The user can read the story onscreen or listen to it on an audio track, so the individual segments usually are relatively short. They can be embellished with graphics and audio, but they work basically as branching versions of traditional narrative writing.

Interactive Movies

Interactive movies can be written for theaters where the choices are made by audience participation (controls located at each seat gather audience reactions and are fed to a computer). The computer averages the response and chooses the reel that shows the selected plot path. Alternatively, interactive movies can be written as CD-ROM or online applications.

The simplest CD-ROM version actually consists of a movie shot with many different plot paths, possibly from the user's point of view. The user is offered choices at various junctures in the plot and is given a chance to respond by clicking on one of a series of possible responses offered in text on the screen. Once a choice is made, the appropriate next section of video is shown. It is possible to record the choices and have the user play back the entire story as a fluid beginning-to-end narrative.

When writing interactive movies, it is possible for the writer to envision a single "correct" version of the narrative and then supply many variants, sometimes tragic, sometimes comic, sometimes lengthy, sometimes very short. Unfortunately, this approach is often unsatisfying to the user because the story's interactivity is simply an overlay superimposed upon a linear narrative. The variants are often just gimmicks offered to show off the interactivity.

As with interactive novels, an interactive movie's writing must stand on its own and the story must be compelling. The interactivity must not be a gimmick, or the user will tire of it easily once the novelty has worn off.

Hybrids

Hybrids offer some of the best creative opportunities for writers. Here the user is presented with any combination of text, video, audio, and game play. The writer can present video screens that appear at various points to advance the plot and/or offer the user choices. Graphics can play a major role in either the overall environment or the page layout. They can be photorealistic, or they can conjure up a fantasy environment. The writer can creatively employ virtually any media element and create very imaginative stories.

Interactivity can serve plot advancement or it can be used in other ways, such as allowing the user to collect information from the content in the environment. This collection can be accomplished through any graphic device—for example, the user can open a suitcase or play back a video through a graphic representation of a VCR and a TV. The information can be used to solve puzzles or just for the user's reference. In educational titles, users may collect information as they advance through the plot so that they can print it out at the end or just refer back to it. This material also can be used for quizzes or recaps throughout the title or at its end.

Game play can be incorporated into the title's narrative by providing a limited and focused game, which can be of the hand-eye coordination or puzzle-solving type. The outcome of the game can determine plot branching or other interactive elements.

Nonnarrative Stories

Nonnarrative stories generally provide many creative uses of multimedia to enhance the environment and to propel the user through the limited "plot." These can take the form of hidden notes, TV or radio "transmissions," audio, animation, rollovers, hidden hot spots, and so on.

The nonnarrative "story" is perhaps the newest and thus far most successful of all interactive fiction. As exemplified by *Myst*, this genre provides a complex and detailed back story that includes an elaborate graphical environment through which the user moves. There is no narrative to speak of, but the user has escape as a goal. Clues are provided throughout in imaginative and graphically creative ways. These clues relate to the back story, which the user learns in bits and pieces, and they also provide information about the environment. The user navigates through the graphic environment by clicking on various hot spots, which move him or her through elaborate scenery that is highly evocative and produces a mood of mystery. Interactive storytelling, as in *Myst*, demonstrates that great complexity can be achieved, so that the user is drawn into a world that is distinctly apart from the real world—and that is exactly the goal of any good storyteller.

Pitfalls

Writers unfamiliar with this territory often make common mistakes. Here are a few pointers:

- *Use organic interactivity.* The biggest mistake writers make in the new media is superimposing interactivity on a linear narrative. This is often done by envisioning the narrative first, then trying to make it interactive. Users are rarely fooled and will lose interest rapidly unless the interactivity flows organically from the narrative.
- *Know the technology.* Writers must not embark on a technological tour de force that will make demands on the hardware system far beyond its capabilities. For example, don't use video where the system's bandwidth is limited (as it is online).
- *Know the venue.* Writers must understand the difference between the theatrical or televised presentation and the home-based CD-ROM. Refer to Chapter 16 for more details.
- *Know the audience and the market.* The audience and market for your title must coincide with the installed base for the hardware platform for which it is written. Unlike traditional books, the user can't just go into a store, buy it, and start reading. The writer must know how many potential purchasers are users of the various computer platforms. This doesn't mean that the writer must keep creativity in check, but there must be some rational relationship between the cost of a title and its potential financial return. Most screenwriters wouldn't write an expensive, extravagant special-effects movie that would only appeal to Druids, would they? Well, maybe. . . .
- *Plan carefully.* Interactive fiction requires detailed planning ahead of time. Unlike a traditional book, interactive media authoring often requires a team effort and blueprints to guide all the team members. Even a single author, who is also an experienced programmer, will need these blueprints to follow, because without them he might get himself into a position from which it can be very costly and time consuming to extricate himself.

Summary

Creativity should not be dampened just because we have outlined some rules. These rules are presented to help create a framework within which writers can be more creative. Interactive fiction can be written in several different formats, including interactive novels, interactive movies, hybrids, and nonnarrative stories. Each has its own special advantages and disadvantages for writers.

There are certain pitfalls you should avoid when you write interactive fiction. You should know the technology, the venue, and the audience and market for your interactive titles, and you should plan carefully in advance.

Part Five

The Technology of Interactive Publishing

20

In and Out of the System

Knowledge is of two kinds. We know a subject ourselves, or we know where we can find information upon it.

—Samuel Johnson

Ebook interactivity requires that the information will be in digital form, and that in turn requires that the information be available to the user for manipulation, and possibly even for inclusion in the user's own works. It may be more of a decision for the publisher than for the writer, but early in the development of a title will come the choice of whether to let the user download or print the information contained in the title. We won't deal with the legal issues in this chapter, but there are other practical matters that writers must consider. Specifically at issue is the way the user will extract information for further use.

With traditional print publishing, ownership is only an issue when one considers photocopying. Because that is an external procedure, it is not an issue for the writer. But interactive systems are digital, and that puts the content into a form that can be directly processed by the very device that is designed to convey it to the reader in the first place. In short, if you can read it on the screen, you can manipulate it, combine it, send it over telephone lines, put it into transportable form via a floppy or optical disc, or print it.

Printing

Software can be written to allow the user to print out an entire section or just what has been selected. In some instances, the user can collect all the information while exploring the title and then print it all out at once. For example, Web browsers today have a Print button at the top of the screen.

If clicked, this button will cause the computer to send the currently viewed page to the printer. Clearly, many users find this immensely useful. To preserve copyright, many publishers of CD-ROMs automatically insert a copyright notice into the program so that anything that is printed contains the copyright information. Web pages can do this as well. In addition, software is available that will "watermark" Web pages, embedding identifying data to prove ownership.

It is possible to preserve the typography of the printed material so that it closely represents the image on the computer screen, or the printed material can be set in any other type. Images may or may not be printable. In fact, it is possible to control all aspects of printing

- Whether any printing is allowed
- Whether users will be allowed to print parts of an article or only the entire article
- Whether typography is preserved
- Whether images can be printed
- Whether a copyright notice will be presented

Users can circumvent all of this by using the Print Screen function available in the Windows and Macintosh operating systems. This will capture whatever is on the screen and send the image to the printer. However, even this capability may be defeated through programming.

These are all functions of programming and publisher policy, but writers should understand these issues and have some familiarity with their potential in the same way that they understand layout and typography in the print media.

Copying

More troublesome for the writer than printing is the user's ability to copy all or part of an ebook title or Web page. Copying means that the user has captured the ASCII code for the letters and can directly insert them into a word processing document. Once in a word processor, the content can be manipulated, reworked, and combined with other works, then published in any medium including other electronic media or print. As noted, many electronic publishers automatically insert copyright notices into copied selections for their titles, but because these are also in digital form, they can be easily removed by the user with a word processing program or any text editor.

As with many of the issues surrounding digital media, these must be weighed against the benefits of making information available to students, researchers, and others who legitimately need it. The benefits of easily transportable information are enormous. People with a family member who suffers from Alzheimer's disease can locate information about the disease on the Web or a CD-ROM, and they can copy it and mail (or e-mail) it to their family doctor for comment. Similarly, a student can research nanotechnology and integrate it into class notes or a research paper. In these cases, the information has amassed value by its electronic availability.

Annotation

We stated earlier that the best interactive material builds upon the best features of a book without losing any of the book's other inherent benefits. One thing you can do with a book is dog-ear the pages and make notes in the margins (unless it's a library book). Interactive media can provide much the same benefit by the inclusion of an annotation feature. Users may be able to insert notes, use electronic versions of yellow "sticky notes," highlight text in yellow (or any other color), or insert "bookmarks." These features are very useful tools for user input, but they fall short of the tactile impression of a real dog-eared page or a physical bookmark.

However, the user will enjoy the unique benefits of the digital system: Notes can now be located instantly by including them in the search function. The ability to locate any note by inputting a word in a search field means that many more notes can be used (because they can be so easily located). The notes can be printed out either in context or together on a separate page. These features add another dimension to interactive media that further strengthens the bonds between the content and the user.

Summary

The user has two primary ways of extracting information from interactive content (other than viewing it directly from the screen): printing it and copying it. Both methods can be controlled via programming, but copying can be more insidious because the user can manipulate the writer's work.

Annotation provides some of the functionality of the printed book by furnishing many ways for the user to add notes and highlights to the text. These functions can be electronically enhanced to include search capability.

21

CD-ROM versus Online

Science and technology multiply around us. To an increasing extent they dictate the languages in which we speak and think. Either we use those languages, or we remain mute.

—J. G. Ballard

Today the world of interactivity is divided into two different paradigms: distributed media (which includes CD-ROMs and floppy discs) and online (which includes private online systems called intranets and the public Internet/World Wide Web). Each has technological advantages and disadvantages, and each is rapidly developing in new and unexpected ways, but writers should be aware that for the time being these two media are very different and serve different purposes.

A Tale of Two Paradigms

The CD-ROM format is self-contained and distributed in the same manner as paper books and audio recordings. In contrast, online systems are more akin to broadcasting in that the content originates from the publisher's location and is accessed by the user from a distance. The standard CD-ROM can contain approximately 650 megabytes of digital information, which can be in the form of text, audio, video, and/or computer programming in any combination. The newer DVD-ROM can store up to 4.7 gigabytes, and a dual-layer single-sided disc can hold 8.5 gigabytes (higher density versions of DVD can accommodate up to 17 gigabytes). Table 21.1 shows the capacity of CD-ROM and DVD-ROM for each of the media. Storage capacity of each disc is large but finite; in some cases, titles are placed on multiple discs and CD-ROM changers are used to access the contents more easily. Online storage capacity is limited to what

Table 21.1 The capacity of CD-ROM and DVD-ROM for each of the media.

	CD-ROM	DVD-ROM
Digital Capacity	650 Mbytes	4.7 Gbytes (single-sided, single-layer)
Text	170,000 pages (single-spaced)	1.2 million pages (single-spaced)
Images	3,250 images (200 kbytes each)	23,500 images (200 kbytes each)
Audio	74 minutes (CD)	535 minutes (CD)
Video (MPEG-1)	74 minutes (MPEG-1)	535 minutes
Video (MPEG-2)	NA	135 minutes

is available in a particular computer, but networked computers provide a theoretically infinite capacity. On the other hand, online media suffer greatly from bandwidth constraints.

Bandwidth: The Diameter of the Pipe

To understand the real difference between CD-ROM and online inter-activity, you must understand the concept of bandwidth. If you think of digital information as water, then bandwidth can be considered as the diameter of a water pipe. If you must fill up a gallon container it would be helpful if you had a wide-diameter pipe, because the container would fill faster. If the pipe had a narrow diameter, it would take longer to fill the container.

Digital information travels through circuits very much like water flows through pipes. Inside a computer these pipes are very wide, so the digital information flows very quickly. However, online systems use phone lines and other communications lines that vary in width but are all still very thin compared to the circuits inside a computer. When we discuss the pipes' width, we use the term *bandwidth*. Online systems provide much lower bandwidth than a computer's internal circuits, and they are a limiting factor in the transfer of information. Bandwidth is often characterized as "bits per second." For example, a modem may allow data to move at a speed of 56.6 kbps, or 56.6 thousand bits per second. While that is fairly fast for low-bandwidth material such as ASCII text, it is agonizingly slow for larger files that contain images, audio, and motion video materials.

In CD-ROM technology, the computer's ability to read the digital data from a disc into its own system is limited primarily by the output transfer rate of the CD-ROM drive. This rate is often specified in terms of "bytes per second" where one byte contains eight bits. Nominally, a CD drive permits a rate of 150 kbytes/second. In most cases, the CD-ROM drive spins at a faster rotational speed, permitting data to flow more quickly from the disc. For example, in a quad-speed CD-ROM drive, the transfer rate is 600 kbytes/second. The speed of operation of a CD-ROM drive is also affected by the time needed to access a particular piece of information on a disc. For example, access time may be 150 milliseconds. The bottom line: CD-ROM is much faster than modem connections and most other online communications systems.

Multimedia must move a very high volume of digital information very quickly so that video images move on the screen and audio flows continuously. Multimedia therefore requires a very high bandwidth. Unfortunately, online systems have not caught up with the CD-ROM's capability to deliver multimedia efficiently. For this reason, although they are steadily improving, online systems are not as good as CD-ROMs for delivering multimedia-rich titles.

However, CD-ROM technology does not offer the opportunity for immediate publication and continuous revision that online does. A multimedia CD-ROM has a production cycle that can take up to a year from concept to distribution. Once it is distributed, it cannot be revised. In contrast, online distribution can be as immediate as a newspaper and can be revised continuously. Writers of time-sensitive information such as current events should lean towards online publishing.

Television versus Print

Since its introduction in 1984, CD-ROM has developed into a rich inter-active multimedia delivery system, and it has attracted talent from other media. For example, CD-ROM design and production has been greatly influenced by a movie and television design sensibility. However, online systems, because they tend to feature less multimedia, have developed into a print-influenced medium. Designers and producers tend to be people with backgrounds in magazine and other print media design; they tend to think in terms of page layout, and have a strong sense of typography and visual aesthetics. For writers, this means that a magazine and book background will tend to be more useful to them in the online world than working with CD-ROMs.

It is important to note, however, that the technology of the World Wide Web has progressed quickly and now provides much more multimedia capability than when it was introduced. One of the earlier problems with multimedia was that its files had to exist on the user's machine before they could begin playing; for example, a video file would have to be downloaded into the user's computer in its entirety before it could be played. The user would have to wait from ten minutes to an hour for just a few minutes of video. However, technology has been introduced that allows the video and audio to "stream." This means that it can begin playing after only a very small portion of the file has been downloaded. After that, it plays as it comes into the computer over the network.

The Online Revolution

The creation of the World Wide Web has extended and amplified the desktop publishing revolution. Desktop publishing lets anyone create a professional-looking publication without the thousands of dollars of equipment previously needed to typeset and print it. But desktop publishing does not provide a distribution mechanism. With the World Wide Web, anyone can write, edit, design, and publish, and the public has instant access to it. There is no paper and there is no limit to the writer's ability to continuously edit the end product. In fact, writers can easily become publishers themselves.

Of course, just as with the desktop publishing revolution, Web technology has made it almost *too* easy to publish. With the traditional publishing model, the writer had to seek out a publisher who was willing to take the risk and make the editorial judgment to bring a manuscript or magazine article to the market. This meant that there was a certain quality filter at work. Today, if anyone can publish, many who shouldn't, will. And once the material is available through the Web, it is as accessible as any other publication.

Money, Money, Money

Every mass medium must have some way for generating revenue for those who take the financial risks and the burden of underwriting the costs. This is another way of saying that there's no such thing as a free lunch. To put it bluntly, if you can't make money at it, what's the point? CD-ROM publishing has already entered the mainstream retail market along fairly predictable lines. While the economic model of online publishing is continuously evolving, it is likely that the Web will be supported by:

- Advertisers (just like magazines and broadcast television)
- Subscriptions (just like magazines and cable and satellite television)
- Commerce (just like catalogues and the at-home shopping channels)

Other economic models are sure to evolve as well

What this means to the writer is that you can publish online on your own, which may be creatively fulfilling but not very remunerative, but there also will be publishers and others who will underwrite the ventures and pay you for your work. This publishing hierarchy is already in place and developing into a model somewhat akin to that of newspapers, magazines, and television journalism.

How to Write for Online

Because online publishing follows the print paradigm more closely than other forms of interactive media, such as CD-ROM, it may be easier for writers to adjust their writing styles for it. Here are some guidelines to follow when you shift to online writing. Many of the guidelines for online writing are based on the general rules for interactive writing already discussed:

- *Write less.* People don't like to read long sections of text on their computer screens.
- *Write concisely.* Write in short interrelated chunks that can link easily with each other.

- *Write with sidebars.* Sidebars are even better online than they are in print. In print, sidebars can confuse the reader because they don't flow logically into and out of the main article. Online, the user makes the choice, and these links build a rich tapestry of interrelated information.
- *Link freely.* Any time you reference something that needs elaboration that might already be available online, look it up and insert links to the other material.
- *Use pictures and multimedia sparingly.* Pictures and multimedia elements can take a long time to load. They will slow the reader down frustratingly.
- *Use tables of contents.* In online publishing, you can put your chapters or topics up front and let the user go directly to his or her points of interest.
- *Allow searching.* This is fundamental. Searching provides the best use of the interactive media because it enriches content by allowing instant access to it.

Selecting Online Content

Almost anything you can write can be published effectively online. Nonfiction subjects work well online—the best subject areas are academic (such as science, history, literature and the arts, geography, and sociology), popular culture (such as television, movies, fashion, travel), and politics and current events. Online fiction is perhaps more challenging because of the resistance some people have to reading on-screen entertainment. However, the chances are that if you can think of it, you can find an audience for it online.

Sometimes online content requires extensive design and engineering, as with an elaborate commercial Web site. In other cases, the publication is very simple and costs nothing more than the writer's time and some inexpensive authoring software. In more elaborate sites, there may be more interactivity or more multimedia. The writer may be asked to provide specific subjects of specific lengths as well as multimedia assets. Other times, if writers are established in print, they may be asked to duplicate their print style online. In such cases, writers of newspaper and magazine pieces may find that the online versions are exactly the same as the print versions. Generally, however, online publishers strive to develop materials that are more than simply reprinted from paper origins.

CD-ROM Lives!

CD-ROM still beats online when it comes to multimedia, design, and interactivity. Online tends to use less "drag and drop" to achieve interactive involvement between the user and the content, but this is changing as the two media converge.

Some CD-ROM titles employ a hybrid approach. They contain online access so that the main content is on the disc but updates can be accessed online. This has been done with CD-ROM encyclopedias, such as Microsoft's *Encarta* and other reference works. This works well with material that already exists but must be supplemented or updated on a continuing basis.

We have seen CD-ROM products that feature a photographic-quality virtual reality environment, while actions taken by the user initiate online hyperlinks. The high bandwidth necessary to provide the virtual reality is delivered from the CD-ROM, and clicking on any object within the virtual world links you back to a Web site that provides timely information (such as price and availability) about the object.

Online Evolves

The bandwidth limitations of online are rapidly eroding. This is happening on two fronts: The pipes themselves are getting wider as new technologies increase the amount of data that can be transmitted over wires, cables, and via satellites; simultaneously, new technologies are being developed that lessen the need for high bandwidth. For example, software like Sun Microsystems' Java programming language or Microsoft's ActiveX technology allows information to be processed efficiently once it arrives on the user's computer instead of prior to transmission. These programs require very little bandwidth, and when they are downloaded into the user's computer they can create miniature applications (called "applets") that allow much of the data to be manipulated in a sophisticated way on the user's computer without any additional bandwidth usage. Bandwidth-heavy programs or artificial environments can be used over and over once the program has been downloaded into the remote computer. At their simplest, these applications can provide interactive financial planning and tax advice, or stock quotes that animate across the page in a marquee.

For example, the software code for a crossword puzzle could be downloaded quickly then compiled into a program that runs on the user's computer; correct words could be shown in blue and incorrect words in red as the user enters them into the puzzle, and the program could provide clues when the user points to any down or across set of spaces. More complex examples of these applets can provide complete interactive programming, animation, three-dimensional gaming, and more.

With the pipes getting wider and the bandwidth requirements getting smaller, there will come a time when the functional distinction between online and CD-ROM is nonexistent. Also, the large bandwidth requirements of audio and video are increasingly reduced through the use of data compression technologies. These systems reduce the amount of data necessary to play sounds or construct moving video images by eliminating redundant or perceptually insignificant information. For example, rather than repeatedly sending out entire images representing each frame of video, video compression algorithms only periodically send fully detailed frames, and primarily send only the changes from one frame to the next.

Summary

CD-ROM is a high-bandwidth, self-contained, long publication process medium, while online is a low-bandwidth, immediate publication process medium. CD-ROM is well suited to highly interactive multimedia titles that don't require immediate publication. Online works well with material that is highly volatile, such as news and current events, and does not require too much multimedia and interactivity.

22

Issues for Writers on the World Wide Web

Experience is never limited, and it is never complete; it is an immense sensibility,
a kind of huge spider-web of the finest silken threads suspended in the chamber
of consciousness, and catching every air-borne particle in its tissue.

—Henry James

Untangling the World Wide Web

The Internet has been around since 1969, when the U.S. Department of Defense created a network of four computers in California and Utah that would be resistant to large-scale damage, such as could be caused by a nuclear war. The early Internet was a relatively crude system for transmitting text and binary files (programs) over telephone lines. Since the Internet's original users were academics and the military, there was no need to make the communication entertaining or visually appealing.

The early Internet required a knowledge of arcane commands in the user-hostile Unix operating system. However, the network's proportions grew steadily and it was eventually partitioned into military and civilian use, with the National Science Foundation forming the high-speed backbone of the United States portion of the network. Internet connections, users, and traffic increased steadily until the Internet became the largest computer network in the world, conveying thousands of applications and countless billions of bytes daily.

With the popularity of GUIs (*Graphical User Interfaces*, pronounced "Gooies") such as the Windows and Macintosh operating systems, users needed a way to communicate over the Internet without using a command line interface. They also needed a way to display text and graphics in an easy-to-navigate point-and-click interface. This need was met in March

1989. Working at CERN (the European Particle Physics Laboratory in Geneva), Tim Berners-Lee proposed a system that would allow scientists to use the Internet to peruse colleagues' research papers; moreover, documents could be placed on individual servers around the network. He called the system the *World Wide Web* (WWW or "the Web" for short), and it was publicly announced and made available on the Internet in August 1991.

The system included a standardized way to tag the various parts of a document to enable software readers to distinguish between a headline, the body text, and other parts of the document. In addition, importantly, the system provided ways to link one part of a document to another part, and one document to another, even if they resided on different servers. This system of putting tags into documents for this purpose is called *HTML* (HyperText Markup Language). HTML, by the way, was adapted from a system called *SGML*, which stands for Standard Generalized Markup Language. SGML was developed to provide a standard way to format documents so that they could be searched more easily by search engines.

By January 1993 there were 50 Web servers on the Internet; however, although CERN had specified ways to share and link documents, both client and reader software was largely undeveloped and definitely user-unfriendly. This changed in February 1993, when Joe Hardin and Marc Andreesen, working at the National Center for Supercomputing Applications at the University of Illinois, created the world's first graphical Web browser, called Mosaic. For the first time, there was a Web browser that supported multimedia applications and was easy to use. Later, Andreesen joined with James H. Clark, the founder of Silicon Graphics Inc., to form Netscape Communications Corporation.

Today, thousands of Web servers are added to the Internet every day, and Netscape's Navigator is battling with Microsoft's Internet Explorer browser for Web supremacy. This competition has pushed these software programs into new and innovative areas; HTML has been expanded greatly and it allows many features, such as e-mail, 3D graphics, live audio and video, phone chat, and white boards, that did not appear in the original version. Fortunately, these two Web browsers are compatible in most ways, and Web pages can be read by either browser.

So, what is the World Wide Web? Actually, it is nothing more than the combination of all the documents that are formatted using HTML, can be viewed by a Web browser, and are transmitted over the Internet. However, you don't even need the Internet to use this system: You can use a Web browser, you can tag your documents in HTML, and you can connect two computers in your home or office and voila—instant home-brewed Internet! Actually, technically this would be an InTRAnet because it does not transmit over the Internet's telecommunications lines. As a matter of fact, you can tag a document using HTML and view it on your computer using a Web browser without transmitting it at all. You could even put together a CD-ROM with a series of linked HTML documents and use a Web browser to view them.

URLs and Home Pages

As with the telephone system, the World Wide Web has its own way of providing users with the Web's equivalent of telephone numbers or addresses. These locating codes are called *URLs* (*Universal Resource Locators*). They contain first the name of the Web's transmission protocol, which is *HTTP* (for *Hypertext Transfer Protocol*); then usually (but not necessarily) *WWW*, which stands for World Wide Web; then the name of the institution that owns the home page, followed by the standard institution type code (com for company; edu for educational institution; gov for government; net for network; mil for military) or, if outside the United States, a two-letter country code (for example, fr for France). Finally, the code has the full path statement (computer-ese for where a particular document is located on the computer) and the particular file name. All of this is separated by the necessary punctuation, which is recognized by the various computers on the entire system. Thus, a typical URL will look something like this:

http://www.imergy.com/index.html

This URL will take you to the home page of a company called Imergy on the World Wide Web. So, we can see that as you dial a phone number to reach any phone in the world, you can type a URL into your Web browser and get to any home page on the Web. Actually, you can get to any document on any computer on the Web, whether or not it is a home page. So this leads us to ask: What exactly is a home page?

The Grammar of the Home Page

To truly answer this question, we need first to understand that the Web does not recognize pages as we know them. Pages refer to paper—something that does not exist in the world of the Web. The Web is designed for display on computer monitor screens (however, you have the option of printing out hard copies of the screens). Because computers allow the user to scroll up and down and from side to side, we can easily display more than can fit on one screen; hence, there is no real use for the concept of a page. However, the Web uses pages to indicate discrete units of information.

The home page is the first or opening page of a Web site that houses a collection of linked pages. The home page serves as a combination book jacket, title page, and table of contents. It is the point of departure for all navigation within the site. It can be limited to the dimensions of the computer screen, or it can be very long, requiring considerable scrolling to get to the end. In fact, a home page may be the entire Web site. The user navigates by clicking hot links within the text or within graphics. In addition, the user can use the navigation controls that are part of the Web browser itself.

The Web browser, as we've seen, is the software program that allows users to view the pages on the Web. It essentially consists of a large screen area in which the content of particular Web pages appears and a navigation area that has control buttons that allow the user to move through the site in various ways. Figures 22.1 and 22.2 show the Netscape Web browser and the Microsoft Internet Explorer Web browser.

Although the designs of home pages are changing and will continue to change rapidly, they all generally contain certain common elements:

- *Navigation.* In its table of contents function, the home page usually has links to other main sections of the Web site. Subsequent locations on the site usually have a Home button to allow users to go directly back to the home page. This is designed so that users will not have to repeatedly click on the Back button.
- *Feedback.* This is an email function built into most web browsers. By clicking on the Feedback button or menu item on the home page,

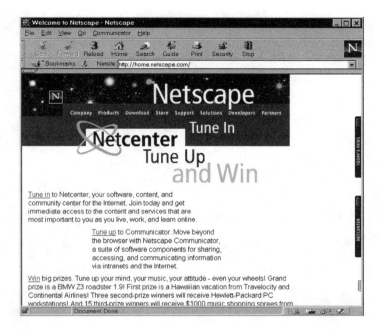

Figure 22.1 Netscape Browser.

the user is able to send e-mail to the person responsible for the home page (this can be the Webmaster or someone involved in the technological aspects of the home page).

- *Search.* Some Web sites provide an internal search engine that is available to the user. This search is confined to the site itself and thus helps ensure that users will not stray onto other sites. Alternatively, some Web sites are home to specific search engines that are designed to locate and display links to other sites.
- *Access Control.* Some Web sites require passwords for user access. In this case they will generally contain fields where the user can enter a password. These home pages usually also provide a registration form with which the user can provide information to the Web site owner.

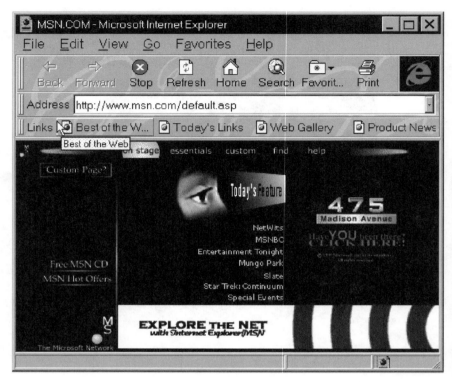

Figure 22.2 Internet Explorer
Browsers are programs used for viewing documents on the World Wide Web. Because each browser decodes the Web's content slightly differently, content on the Web will look different depending on which browser is used.

Layout

The technical issues that determine the way the Web browser displays its content present challenges and opportunities for the design of material presented on the Web. To understand this, it is necessary to understand how the Web browser deals with its content.

Interpreted Functional Typography

The Web browser, as we've seen, reads content formatted with HTML. HTML is an interpreted and functionally oriented formatting language.

This means that the text, when formatted in HTML, is separated into its *functional* parts, which the browser interprets to assign the correct typography.

For example, a document might have first, second, and third level headings and subheadings, body text, bullet lists, and numbered lists, in addition to graphics. When such a document is marked up with HTML codes, only the *level* of the headings and the *existence* of the body text and the other elements are indicated, using codes called "tags." These tags identify these parts of the documents for the browser, but the browser itself determines how they are displayed.

Thus, the various levels of the headlines, the typography of the body text, the styles of the bullets in the lists, and so on will look different from browser to browser. This is true even for the same types of browsers. This is because users can control the way their particular browser displays body text, headlines, and other elements. In addition, users can set the overall width of the browser to any desired dimension. This means that the typography and the layout cannot be easily controlled by the publisher or writer.

To get around this, many Web publishers use graphics to display headlines and other text. If they set the type as a picture and tell the browser where to display that picture, then that type will always be displayed as intended because the browser treats it as a picture. The problem with this approach is that pictures are slow to load and they are an inefficient use of bandwidth. Also, it is difficult to display text in columns on the Web, although it is possible to use them by tricking the browser into thinking they are tables. (Text can be placed in tables and the tables can be set not to display borders.) Of course, snaking columns don't work too well because they require that the user scroll down to the bottom, then up to the top again, in an awkward pattern.

Despite the limitations of the Web, problems can be surmounted and more importantly, can be used to advantage. Advances in the basic technology have enabled many Web publishers to emulate the print page, but it is questionable whether this is desirable. One style that has been used to great effect on journalistically oriented pages is the narrow column of text with pull quotes and hot links placed to the left of the columns. The narrow text column provides a good flow of information that can be read in a continuous stream. The pull quotes and interactive links on the left side are less intrusive than they would be if they interrupted the flow of the main text. At the same time, they provide audio and video quotes that embellish the main text (especially useful in journalism) and links to side-bars and related articles. This departure from the print metaphor works well on a computer monitor.

Web Journalism

Newspapers and magazines benefit greatly from the technology of the Web. Because it uses a text-based paradigm, it fills the role of print journalism nicely, but because it can contain multimedia elements and is immediately delivered to the user, it provides the benefits of television and radio. But the real reason the Web is such an advance over television, radio, and print is that it is interactive. The obvious use of inter-activity in journalism is the linking of the source material with journalists' reporting. The story can refer to a speech, and the user can hear the speech at will (or choose to ignore it, or listen to only a portion of it). Short audio and video clips can enhance the story, while links to sidebars, related stories, and interpretations of the event further enhance the reporting.

The ability to link the home site with other relevant sites rounds out the enrichment of the user's experience. Users can read the story, with all its enriching sound, audio, and hyperlinks, and at the same time have access to the source of the quotations, statistics, and other background.

What does this mean for the writer? How do traditional print journalists adjust their style to the Web? The transition from traditional journalism to the Web is no less profound than the transition from print to television journalism. The writer needs to understand that the story will have greater and more immediate impact for the user. The writer must provide a firm context for the story and allow the user to pick up important facts from hyperlinks and multimedia elements.

The writer will need to do more interpretation for the user, while the medium itself provides most of the factual context, but the writer often will have to provide the links to the source material and thus the background of the story. Writers will have to be aware of important research sources not only for their writing, but to provide links for the user. The writer must also understand that some users will not return to the story. They will get lost on the Web in other sites that may be more interesting to them. Thus, writers will need to develop a solid Web-oriented style that will keep the users coming back to the original story.

One way to do this is to keep the story as short and as compelling as possible. Editors will need to keep the support material on the home Web site and to gently guide the user back to the original material through the use of good navigation and strong interactive design.

Of course, the Web allows many functions that are impossible in either newspapers or television. A short list of these includes:

- The ability to search a Web site or the entire WWW instantly.
- Crossword puzzles that show clues in the puzzle diagram and score themselves.
- Instant weather information with satellite photos and diagrams that can be customized for the user's geographic area.
- Interactive maps that allow the user to input a person's or company's name and have the address displayed in the appropriate location.
- Personalized home pages that automatically find subjects of interest and set out a personal daily newspaper based on the user's pre-established profile.
- The ability to send instant email directly to the author, editor, or publisher (instant letters to the editor).
- Interactive chat with other users interested in similar topics.

Content Automation

One of the early problems faced by Web journalists and editors was that writing HTML was time-consuming; it took too long to get material tagged and ready for publication on a deadline. Today, to keep the delivery of material consistent with the immediate delivery the Web provides, many word-processing programs automatically export HTML documents, and content insertion generally is automated. In this way, a journalist can write a story and publish it on the Web instantly.

Searching

The ability to search the entire Web is an awesome capability that should not be overlooked. It is the existence of these search engines, which are usually free of any cost to the user, that truly unites all of the material on the Web into a single interactive database. There are many different search engines and sites. Most, such as Alta Vista, will perform simple or full Boolean searches. But others, like Yahoo, categorize the material, which makes it easier for some people to use if they have only a general idea of what they want to find.

Proactive Agents and Web Spiders

Computer software sometimes gets so useful that it disturbs some people. There is software that actually looks over your shoulder as you work, and learns how you look things up, and then goes out onto the Web and finds what you want. These programs learn the user's syntax and soon develop the ability to duplicate the way a particular user will phrase a search request, or it will keep track of the subjects on which a particular user has performed searches, and then automatically searches the Web and finds subjects that match. These programs are called *proactive agents.*

Another type of program that does something similar is a Web spider. This program is like a search engine, but instead of performing a search once it keeps looking for the search term and sends back information to the user about where this information can be found. It does this by following all of the links on the Web, one at a time. If it reaches a dead end (a section that does not contain further links), it retraces its steps and goes on to the next link until it has covered the whole Web. Because the Web is constantly growing, this program is constantly looking. While it looks, it indexes every site and looks for the search term that was specified.

There are many permutations of these programs, but one problem is that as information becomes more valuable, more and more sites will create software gates that keep these programs out. Of course, there is nothing more enticing to a software developer than the forbidden fruit of an inaccessible Web site. While the technical and legal aspects of this unfold, there is much for Web writers to contemplate.

The Web Marches On

The World Wide Web has so exploded in popularity that some studies say that in certain demographic groups, more time is spent in front of a computer screen surfing the Web than in front of a television set. Advertising agencies have discovered the Web and have made it more commercial than even the far-thinking Department of Defense could ever have imagined. Because of concerns about security, commerce was slow to develop on the Web, but that is now quickly changing with the advent of security features.

In fact, new systems for financial transactions may create new opportunities for writers. For example, systems are being developed for small financial transactions, including micropayments involving sums of less than one cent. Before the Web, these transactions were not feasible because credit card companies would not process charges for amounts under ten dollars. But suppose that you are a comedy writer. You could sell a different one-liner every day on the Web and charge each buyer a nickel. Alternatively, a company might collect 0.01 cent each time someone simply clicked on its home page. With enough volume, this could generate serious revenue. And with the ease of publishing on the Web, anyone could do it with a minimal investment.

As technical issues such as the need for increased bandwidth and more universal accessibility are solved, it is likely that the Web and its successors will become a major media phenomenon similar to television. However, the Web will have at least one important difference: Television uses a centralized distribution model that consists of few broadcasters and many viewers. But with the Web, each viewer is potentially also a broadcaster. Desktop publishing, with desktop distribution of books, magazines, newspapers, audio records, videos, and still-to-be-invented vehicles will be open to anyone with Web access. While the expansion and evolution of the distribution model will take some getting used to, it is still the interactivity that sets the Web apart from other media. And it will be those writers who understand the basics of interactivity who will have the best chance of communicating over the new media.

CD-ROM/Web Hybrids

While the Web is evolving, it will continue for at least several years to be limited by relatively low bandwidth when compared to distributed media such as CD-ROMs. To take advantage of the high bandwidth of CD-ROM media and the immediacy of the Web, as we observed in Chapter 21, some CD-ROMs contain links to sites on the Web. The CD-ROM/Web hybrid disc can seamlessly link the Web and the disc's content. In this way, high bandwidth multimedia material can be delivered via CD-ROM, while more timely material can be delivered via the Web.

Losing the Reader on the World Wide Web

Writers often need to adjust to the dynamic nature of interactivity in their writing. This means abdicating a certain amount of control because users will be able to carve out their own pathways through the material. We have seen how interactive media gives the reader the ability to explore material out of order. This means that the writer must understand that the material may or may not be read sequentially. But with the World Wide Web and other hyperlinked online systems, the writer confronts a new risk—that the reader will depart from the writer's material altogether and will begin exploring totally different content from a completely different source. Because the Web allows the writer (or the writer's editor) to place links to other information on the Web within any material, the user may begin to read the writer's material, hyperlink to another (and possibly contradictory) piece of material, and never return to the point of origin.

Suppose, for example, that you have written a study of extremist political groups in America and their usage of new media. To illustrate a point, you might quote from some neo-Nazi manifesto. In traditional linear writing, the reader would be brought back to your text immediately after reading the excerpt. But on the Web, to prove the point, you may link to the home page of a neo-Nazi group. While this may illustrate the point at hand perfectly, there is no built-in mechanism for bringing the reader back. The new page might contain links that catch the reader's attention, and the reader may get lost on the Web, or at least lose interest in the original thesis. More importantly, the boundary between your writing and the hyperlink will be indistinct to the reader. Material may flow seamlessly between the two sources to the reader and the intent of your material may become seriously compromised. That opportunity for self-exploration is perhaps the Web's greatest strength and a writer's greatest challenge.

The Web Gets Pushy

The Web started out as a fully interactive medium. This was because all information that came over the Web had to be requested by the user in order to be received: You selected the Web site or hyperlink you wanted to explore. That all began to change in 1996 when the Pointcast Network debuted its online service. This service consisted of a specialized browser that can be continuously updated with news stories, sports, stock, and other information, which is fed to the browser according to a pre-set profile filled out by the user. The information updates automatically at regular intervals if the user has a permanent network connection, or whenever the user goes online and clicks the Update button. The information is displayed in slick animated graphics that are intermingled with advertising. This is called push technology.

The idea behind push is that information is not fed to the user in response to a request, but as it becomes available. The only interactive action the user performs is to set up some parameters in advance to tell the service what type of information is desired. In this way, the Web has become slightly less interactive and more TV-like.

Advertisers embraced push technology early on because it was familiar territory, following a slightly modified broadcast model. More importantly, as people spend increasing amounts of time in front of their computer screens rather than their TV sets, the competition for eyeballs attracts advertisers to new technologies that can help them get their messages across. Push looks promising because it combines the benefits of the Web with the broadcast capability of TV.

Summary

The World Wide Web is a constantly growing collection of online documents. They are unified because they are all written with HTML tagging, thus allowing Web browsers to display them on a computer screen and move from one document to another. Because Web browsers interpret the different parts of a document and assign their own typography to each element, a document can look quite different on different browsers (or even in the same type of browser with different configurations).

The Web presents many opportunities and challenges for writers. The ability to publish immediately, hyperlink within and outside the original Web site, and provide multimedia creates a dynamic new medium that combines the best of television, radio, and print journalism.

One problem writers must face when writing for the Web is that because their story will link with other Web sites, there is a risk that their story will be linked to contradictory material or that the user will not read their complete story.

As the home page evolves, the convergence between appliances such as TVs, VCRs, CD players, and computers may blur the line between information and entertainment devices. As this happens, we may see URLs become more like broadcast television channels.

23

Very Basically, How Does All This Work?

Sorry to interrupt the festivities, Dave, but we have a problem.
—HAL 9000, Computer (from *2001: A Space Odyssey*)

Even in its most elemental form, storytelling requires knowledge and expertise beyond that of mere yarn-spinning. For example, even the earliest storytellers were surely shrewd observers of human nature, knew their audiences well, and had an inherent sense of theatrics, rhythm, and pacing. As storytelling embraced different means to communicate tales, the extent of its expression increased.

Whereas essential storytelling has not changed much since prehistory, the knowledge needed to convey tales certainly has changed, particularly as computer technology has been adapted to the task. The computer environment is unlike any other, with very specialized technical limitations and user expectations. The more the writer knows about computers, the better.

However—and fortunately—there is a limit to that truism. A complete mastery of computer science is *not* necessary. What *is* necessary is that the writer understands enough about computers so that the resulting title is authored in a way that fully exploits all the power offered by technology, while at the same time making the technology, including its frustrations and limitations, completely invisible to the user. In other words, if the author knows enough about technology, then perhaps the user doesn't have to. A good ebook is one in which the story is enhanced by technology but never hindered by it. Given the tremendous power of computer technology, with both positive and negative results, its effect on new media storytelling is evident.

1 + 0 = 1

As we observed in Chapter 1, a computer is a glorified adding machine. Its ability to add 1 or 0 together is simple, but its other ability, repeating the calculation hundreds of millions of times a second and keeping track of the implications of the calculation, makes it more than a merely novel invention. In fact, from a writer's point of view, computers are inherently much more powerful than printing presses, audio recorders, movie projectors, and any other means of expression. Computers encompass all of those technologies, uniquely consolidate them, and introduce entirely new concepts, such as networks, to yield the most powerful creative means yet invented. Without question, these fast adding machines will revolutionize creative expression, including the creative act of writing.

A computer is not intelligent. It is not smart. It is not your friend, and probably it is not your enemy either. A computer is simply a tool. It can be used constructively or destructively, and the former requires infinitely more expertise than the latter. For best results, a full complement of tools is needed; all workers must make the necessary investment in their toolboxes. A good worker does not blame his or her tools, and a good new media writer does not blame his or her computer. To avoid the need for accusations, a new media writer must know the applications and limitations of computers. A good worker would not use a hammer to drive in a screw. A good new media writer wouldn't put a 500 kbyte picture on a Web page. Above all, the practitioner must have the experience needed to produce the best result possible. It is difficult to write a good book, and it is also difficult to write a good ebook, a difficulty compounded by all the other complexities added by the technology involved. Thus, it is *more* difficult to write a good ebook, and only through hard work and practice can a good result be forthcoming.

No Guts, No Glory

A computer is made up of a number of interrelated systems that combine to make a functioning device that can input data, perform computations, and output a result. The centerpiece of the collection is the CPU (central processing unit); it must direct the operation of the entire system, including memory and input/output. Its inherent design and speed largely determine the perceived power of the computer. Generally, the world of consumer computers is divided into the CPUs made by Intel and found in IBM-type PC computers, and the CPUs made by Motorola and found in Macintosh-type computers. These two processor types are incompatible. Although some Macintosh computers, (such as the PowerPC), will run Intel software, IBM-type computers are limited to Intel-type software. A new media writer generally must choose to write for one platform or another. (In some cases, hybrid titles may be presented on either platform.) Interestingly, either platform can be used as the authoring environment, as can other environments such as Unix systems. Moreover, it is entirely likely that a multimedia title might be the product of different authoring platforms. The choice of authoring platform depends entirely on the particular authoring software used.

Computers are also distinguished by their operating systems. The operating system forms the software basis for a computer, provides the principal user interface, and determines what other application programs (including your ebook) will run on the computer. Operating systems follow the same divide as processors, and in fact the different processors mandate this. Macintosh computers use the Macintosh operating system. IBM-type computers primarily use a Windows/DOS operating system, a product of Microsoft Corporation. A variety of older Windows programs, now collectively known as 3.x, is still in wide use; however, the Windows 95 operating system is a superior product and supersedes 3.x. The new media writer must determine which operating system to embrace. Although dual expertise is certainly possible, realistically, most authors focus their efforts on one. In some cases, the type of computer and operating system makes no difference. As we observed in Chapter 22, Web pages can be written so they are readable on either Macintosh or Windows machines, running different operating systems and different browsers. This is because Web pages are all written according to the HTML standard, and because the TCP/IP protocol, the standard for data transmission over the internet, makes all computers equal in the eyes of the Internet.

Memory

All computers contain memory chips in the form of ROM (read-only memory) and RAM (random-access memory). ROM memory chips contain programs and data that are usually unchanging over the life of the computer, and this information is retained when the computer is turned off. For example, during a power-up sequence they might instruct a computer to bring other programs into operation and supervise other low-level operations. Some computers contain flash ROM memory; it is used to store information that is occasionally updated (for example, to upgrade a utility program). RAM memory is used to store programs and data temporarily during operation; the contents are lost when power is turned off. Modern computers may require 16 or 32 megabytes of RAM, or even more. The amount of RAM determines what programs can run successfully and the program efficiency. For example, if RAM is limited, a program may have to shift data continually between RAM and hard disk memory, thus slowing operation. In most computers, additional RAM can be easily added, at relatively low cost.

Storage Devices

Computers are superb at processing data, but their utility also largely depends on their ability to accept data, store it, and then output it. A wide variety of storage devices have thus been developed; some devices are internal to the computer and are intended for local storage, while others are used to store data externally and to transport it physically. Two types of storage common to desktop computers are hard and floppy disk drives.

All desktop computers contain a hard disk drive. This storage device uses a series of stacked magnetic disks holding 1 or 2 gigabytes, or more, of programs and data in a sealed, nonremovable environment, at extremely low cost. Hard disks offer relatively fast access times and random access. When programs such as the operating system and applications such as word processors are loaded into a computer, they reside physically on the hard disk. Clearly, the capacity of the hard disk determines the size and number of programs that can be stored and operated.

Virtually all computers contain floppy disk drives to store small amounts (1.44 megabytes) of data; while this capacity is sufficient for text files (an entire novel may fit on one floppy) it is insufficient for audio and video files. Many computer users use a variety of external storage devices to overcome the limitations of floppy disks. For example, Zip drives are small portable devices that can record and rerecord 100 megabytes of data. Larger-capacity Jaz drives can hold 600 megabytes of data. These and other storage devices are extremely useful; however, they are not universally found in computers and so may be incompatible among different users. Most applications software and ebook titles are distributed via floppy disk and CD.

Compact Disc Format

The CD format employs a 120-millimeter optical disc that holds approximately 650 megabytes of data. This invention represented a great advance in storage capacity; one CD holds the equivalent of 470 floppy disks, 275,000 pages of alphanumeric data, or 3,600 video images. Digital information is stored on a CD disc in the form of microscopic bumps across a flat surface; the player's laser beam reflects from the surface, and the bumps momentarily decrease the intensity of the reflected light. The changes in intensity are used to denote binary data. The CD is an extremely robust format with a long archival life.

The CD-audio format was originally introduced in 1983 to provide storage and playback of high-quality stereo audio programs of up to 72 minutes, and it has been highly successful in that role. However, the role was expanded in 1984 to include the CD-ROM (read-only memory) format, used to store nonaudio data such as computer programs, text documents, and images. Today, most personal computers contain a CD-ROM drive that can play back these titles and CD-audio discs. Because the data transfer rate of 150 kbytes/second is limited, most CD-ROM drives rotate the disc at a faster rate (such as 8 times) to increase the data transfer rate. This allows more complex programs, such as video files, to be played from a CD-ROM disc. Although its storage capacity is moderately large, CD-ROM disc capacity is too small for large programs or databases. This has led to the advent of CD-ROM changers, as well as the high-density DVD format.

Both the CD-audio and CD-ROM formats are read-only formats in which data is permanently placed on the disc at the time of manufacture. The CD-R format, introduced in 1988, allows users to purchase blank discs and make their own CD recordings using CD-R drives. Any type of digital data (programs, text, audio, or video) may be recorded to a CD-R disc, up to a limit of 650 megabytes. Once the data is recorded, it cannot be erased or altered. In 1996 the CD-RW format was introduced, allowing users to record, play back, erase, and rerecord data, using a CD-RW drive.

DVD Format

The DVD format is the successor to the CD format. DVD was originally the acronym for *Digital Video Disc*; this described the proposed format's ability to play full-motion video files, including feature-length movies. As the format's intended applications mushroomed far beyond simple video storage, the name was dropped; DVD is the format's official name.

DVD provides cross-platform convergence between home entertainment and personal computers. Like the CD, DVD uses a 120-millimeter diameter disc holding digital data. However, a DVD disc may hold 4.7 gigabytes of data on a single layer, and up to 8.5 gigabytes on dual layers read from a single disc side. In addition, the specification allows up to 17 gigabytes on four data layers read through two sides. In any of its densities, a DVD may output data at a rate of 10 Mbps (million bits per second).

DVD-video discs hold feature films; one data layer holds two hours and 13 minutes of video and audio on a single layer, with up to 3 hours, 56 minutes on dual layers, with seamless playback. The video portion is coded with *MPEG-2* (Motion Picture Experts Group) data compression algorithm for video quality that approaches a studio-quality picture; the audio employs Dolby Digital (formerly known as AC-3) to provide 5.1 audio, providing five main channels plus a subwoofer effects channel for surround sound.

DVD-video discs allow multiple aspect ratios so that content providers can code fully compatible 4:3 conventional pan and scan, 16:9 widescreen, or letterbox display from a single disc. A ratings control provides parental lockout features. Content providers can code up to eight independent language tracks and up to 32 independent sets of subtitle texts.

DVD-video also allows multiple story lines so that content providers can code true interactivity and alternate story lines to provide different movie versions. In addition, the format allows multiple camera angles so that content providers can code up to nine different camera angles for each scene. DVD-video players may also play CD-audio discs.

The DVD-ROM format features applications for computer software, multimedia titles, games, and other wide-bandwidth computer programs that demand fast data transfer. DVD movie discs will play on PCs fitted with a DVD-ROM drive. Other DVD formats include DVD-audio (players and audio discs with sound quality beyond CD-audio); DVD-R (players and discs for recording write-once discs); and DVD-RAM (players and discs for rerecording data). In addition, the circuits used to decode DVD signals conceptually encompass those used in direct broadcast satellite and cable boxes; in addition, DVD circuits could be used to run a multimedia Internet browser. Thus, in the future one DVD component could be used to perform all of these functions.

User I/O and Peripherals

Many computers are embedded into systems so that users never directly see or use them; for example, computers regulate automobile engines to optimize performance while restricting fuel emissions. However, most computers used to replay ebook titles are equipped for direct user control. In most cases, the controllers and displays are ubiquitous: the QWERTY keyboard, mouse, or trackball, and CRT or LCD screen. In most cases, the writer need not be overly concerned about variations and quality differences. However, it is worth noting that the resolution of video displays does vary, and care must be taken not to convey too much detail to the screen.

This is particularly true in Web page authoring; increasingly, consumers use Web TV devices to view pages and standard television sets as their viewers. Whereas most computer screens provide crisp SVGA resolution, television sets cannot accommodate more than lower-quality VGA detail. To be legible via Web TV, you must limit the fine detail on your Web page. Moreover, remember that the TV user will be sitting farther away from the screen than a computer user. In any case, detail increases file size, which leads to slower download times over modems.

A wide variety of peripheral equipment is available for both authoring and replaying ebook titles. Scanners are used to transfer printed material into digital form. For example, still images such as color photographs may be digitized for inclusion in a Web page; scanners are increasingly common and widely used by both professional and amateur authors. Although a scanner works only with still images, it is possible to generate very large files if the original image is physically large and the scanner's resolution is high. For example, you can easily generate files larger than 2 megabytes; this is too large to fit on a floppy disk. Large image files may present bandwidth problems leading to slow downloading times. It is important to limit the dimensions and resolution of the digital image to overcome this problem. In addition, the file format influences file size; for example, JPEG (Joint Photographic Experts Group) video compression is used primarily to reduce the size of still image files. Compression ratios of 20:1 to 30:1 can be achieved with little loss of quality, and much higher compression ratios are possible.

Audio

By definition, all multimedia computers contain a sound card or equivalent circuitry resident on the motherboard. These devices contains a codec (coder/decoder) comprising an analog-to-digital (A/D) and digital-to-analog (D/A) converter so that stereo sound can be input from microphones and line level analog sources and output to speakers.

Audio sampling is data-intensive. The original analog audio waveform is sampled so that individual amplitude points on the waveform are periodically represented as numbers. For good fidelity, the sampling rate should be 44.1 kHz, and each amplitude should be represented as a 16-bit word (yielding a 0–22 kHz frequency response and noise floor of –96 dB). Lower fidelity recording might employ 22 kHz sampling and 8-bit words (yielding a 0–11 kHz frequency response and noise floor of –48 dB). Clearly, higher-fidelity digital recordings mandate large file sizes, and care must be taken to limit audio file sizes. For example, one minute of high fidelity stereo will consume 10 megabytes of memory.

Soundcards are often used in conjunction with audio recording and editing programs. For example, a Windows program called Sound Forge turns a PC into a recording/editing studio and gives a user the ability make truly professional recordings. Recently, the computer industry has adapted the AC '97 Codec standard for sound recording and playback. This standard will increase audio fidelity and add new consumer features as well.

Digital audio file formats allow sound files to be compatibly stored and transmitted; some popular formats include AIFF, SDII, QuickTime, WAVE, JPEG, MPEG, and OMF.

When moving audio files through low-bandwidth channels such as the Web, data compression algorithms are used to remove data that is either considered to be inaudible or simply is less prominent. Using data reduction, audio data rates can be reduced to the extent that reasonable fidelity can be obtained even with real-time streaming. In this way, for example, radio stations can broadcast live programs over the Web. Software players are available as plug-ins for Web browsers.

Most soundcards also contain *MIDI* (Musical Instrument Digital Interface) synthesizers. MIDI does not record and play back actual audio waveforms; instead, it uses a code to control a synthesizer circuit, which synthesizes sounds. MIDI playback thus sounds somewhat artificial. To its credit, MIDI is very efficient in terms of file size. For example, a 3-minute MIDI performance may be stored in a 20-kbyte file.

Video

Video capture cards allow users to input full-motion video signals from sources such as camcorders, edit the program, and reproduce it for recording on the camcorder. Even without a dedicated video capture card, most computers allow playback of video programs. Digital video is similar to digital audio in that analog waveforms must be sampled and measured. However, with digital video much more data is needed. Because a picture is comprised of thousands of pixels, the overall number of bits is very large. For these reasons, video files are among the largest of all computer files. A broadcast-quality video program may require a transfer rate of 200 or 300 Mbps. At 200 Mbps, a CD would store about 26 seconds of program, and a single-speed drive would take 72 minutes to play back those 26 seconds.

Data compression is often used to conserve data in a video file. For example, the data rate may be reduced by a factor of 140:1, leading to a rate of about 1.4 Mbps. In this way, a CD may store 72 minutes of full motion video. Specifically, *Motion JPEG* (MJPEG) may be used to store motion video; this is often used in video editors where individual frame quality is needed. Many proprietary JPEG formats are used. As in the DVD format,

MPEG video compression is often used for motion video, often with accompanying audio. Some frames are stored with great resolution, then intervening frames are stored as differences between frames; video compression ratios of 200:1 are possible. In many applications, however, even this reduction is too little. For example, in Web applications, lower rates are needed to send video files efficiently. Additional data compression must be used, and in addition the picture size is reduced (fewer pixels require less data) and the frame rate is often reduced (instead of 30 frames/second, we might use 15 frames/second). In this way, video files can be moved through low-bandwidth channels, and real-time streaming video can be accommodated as well, albeit with degraded picture quality. As with audio sound-cards, video cards are used in conjunction with software to allow editing, creation of special effects, and other video processing.

QuickTime is an extension to the Macintosh operating system; it is a file format with compression algorithms for processing multimedia files. It can be used to play videos on Macintosh and Windows computers. More generally, time-based files, including audio, animation, and MIDI, can be stored in documents as are text and graphics, and it then can be synchronized, controlled, and replayed.

Because of the time-base inherent in a video program, the video itself can be used to control preset actions. QuickTime movies may have multiple audio tracks; for example, different language soundtracks can accompany a video. Videos can be played on a Macintosh at 15 or 30 frames/second. However, frame rate, along with picture size and resolution, may be limited by hard-disk data-transfer rates.

Hardware and software tools allow the user to record video clips to hard disk in real time, compress video, edit video, add audio tracks, and then play the result as a QuickTime movie. In some cases, the system can be used as an off-line video editor, and the finished product can be output directly to disk or videotape. Audio files with 16-bit, 44.1 kHz quality can be inserted in QuickTime movies; QuickTime also accepts MIDI data for playback.

Modems and Beyond

Many personal computers contain a *modem* (*modulate-demodulator*). This device is used to connect the computer to a network via ordinary telephone lines. To accomplish this, the modem converts computer data to an audio signal (exactly the thing that telephone lines were designed to handle) and transmits it to the phone line; likewise it can receive an audio signal from the line and convert it back into data. This conversion is handled via A/D and D/A converters and the binary data modulates a carrier signal that is audible to humans and thus recognized by telephones. Although modem speed has increased greatly (speeds of 56.6 kbps are now in use) they are still slow; at best, modems are a transition technology. Some users install *ISDN* (Integrated Services Digital Network) lines to support rates of 144 kbps or higher; local telephone companies will provide this service. Cable modems for home use will adapt cable TV systems to send and receive data rates of over 10 Mbps. Many businesses are wired with *LANs* (Local Area Networks) so that users may access *ethernet* or *10base-T* connections using copper cable with a bandwidth of 10 Mbps, or *FDDI* (Fiber Distributed Data Interface) using optical fiber cables with a bandwidth of 100 Mbps.

Nothing But Net

The Internet is a packet-switched network. In the same way that the U.S. Post Office does not need a special truck to send a letter from one address to another, but rather routes the letter through an existing infrastructure, the Internet sends information over its infrastructure according to standardized addresses. A user sends information to a local network, which is controlled by a central server computer. This server uses TCP protocol to parse the information into many smaller pieces, and puts each of them in a packet according to the IP protocol, with the proper address on each packet. The network sends the packets to a router computer, which reads the address and sends the packets over data lines to other routers. Each packet may travel a different route. This helps spread loads across the network but reduces average travel time. Real-time transmission is more difficult because packets may be delivered out of order, delivered multiple times, or dropped altogether. When the packets arrive at the destination address, the information is assembled and acted upon.

The Internet operates on a first-come, first-serve basis; therefore, throughput rate is unpredictable. There is no bandwidth reservation; the Internet cannot guarantee a percentage of the network throughput to the sender. The number of packets delivered per second is continuously variable; memory buffers at the receiver can smooth discontinuities due to bursty delivery, but this adds delay time to the throughput. In addition, the Internet operates point to point; a message addressed to multiple receivers must be sent multiple times; this greatly increases bandwidth requirements for multicasting.

In short, the Internet is quite unlike telephone lines, which establish a temporary but fixed direct connection between two parties (for as long as you care to pay for it). Rather, the Internet is almost organic in the way it moves data from place to place, according to current conditions. If you think the idea of an organic global computer system is a little scary, you're not alone.

The OS/Browser Wars

When the World Wide Web began to explode, only one company had a dominant share of the browser market—Netscape Communications. Microsoft, which controlled the world of IBM-type computers with its DOS operating systems and Windows graphical user interface, was slow to realize the power of the Web. Thus, Netscape was well on its way to owning the browser market when Microsoft finally woke up.

Netscape's response to Microsoft was to infuse its browser with an ever-increasing array of capabilities usually accomplished by the operating system. If they continued in this direction, then Microsoft's DOS/Windows operating system and interface combination would become obsolete: users would only have to plug their Netscape-equipped computers into the network and everything would work without an outside operating system. Talk began to surface of a "Network Computer"—a $500 device that operates from the software it accesses over the network. This was definitely very bad news for Microsoft.

However, with its worldwide dominance over more than 80 percent of personal computers, Microsoft was well positioned to implement a catch-up strategy to include more and more browser functionality into its existing operating system. Microsoft thus has begun to blur the line that divides the operating system from the browser, infusing its Windows system with browser capabilities. As this drama plays out, the outcome will most likely make the Web more accessible to more people in more places around the world.

Summary

Although in theory a new media author need not know computer mechanics to produce good work, in practice familiarity with computers is very important, and in particular authors must become experts in authoring software; the path to this expertise begins with user's manuals and books devoted to specific software programs, and ends only after long hours of study and practice. Ultimately, every new media author learns that the computer environment is different from any other, and new media authors must learn about computers.

On one hand, computers are dumb beasts with no more intelligence than house plants; in fact, they are perhaps even less intelligent. However, with sufficient hardware and software, a computer can give the impression of great brainpower. Most importantly, writers of new media are able to use the power of computers, and avoid their problems, to allow computers to augment their work in the eyes and ears of the user. For example, for a title to appeal to a user its author must consider the storage capacity of distributed media, the bandwidth of data transfers, and the capability of peripheral equipment.

Although all computers, both those used to write work and those used to replay it, are conceptually identical, there are numerous practical differences. The divide between Windows and Macintosh computers is vast, and authors must choose which platform they wish to write for, remembering that the Windows installed base is considerably larger, and growing faster, than Macintosh's.

Whatever the size and scope of the hardware in a particular computer, authors must be very careful to respect the practical limitations of the machines that users will ultimately use to read their works. It is easy to author a great-looking ebook that requires a $5,000 computer for playback. It is much harder to do the same on a $500 computer. Moreover, clearly, the lower the system requirements, the greater your potential audience.

This brings us back to one of the first ideas we discussed in this book. Books require no playback device, and they have many inherent advantages

212 The Technology of Interactive Publishing

over other media that do require technology to be accessed. We must use technology in such a way that its benefits outweigh its constraints. Technology can do wonderful things for the writer and for the user. But writers should be wary of technology even as they embrace it—the most brilliant interactive medium offers nothing if users cannot access it. User access can be denied because of cost, difficulty of navigation, or inadequate distribution. Writers must assess the technology in order to make the best decision about its use. Technology will continue to evolve and writers will always be able to explore these new means of creative expression. We can't wait.

Glossary

ActiveX   A technology promoted by Microsoft for embedding programming within Web pages.

analog   Any means of recording audio or video via a representation of the waveform on the recording medium rather than by converting to numbers. Nondigital.

applet   Small software applications ("applets") that allow data to be manipulated locally on the user's computer, thus decreasing the bandwidth needed to run networked programs.

ASCII (American Standard Code for Information Interchange) A numeric code for each letter, number, and punctuation symbol in English. Material that consists of ASCII code can be manipulated by any word processing program or text editor. Advanced word processing programs insert many codes into documents other than the ASCII codes for the letters, spaces, and punctuation. In order to be used by most programs or transmitted or stored for retrieval, information must be in ASCII code. The letter "A" in ASCII is a number. If it were not converted to a number, it would just be a picture that looks like the letter "A."

assets   The elements of a multimedia project—text, audio, video, artwork, and/or computer-generated pictures that can be integrated or used individually in an electronic product or service.

authoring   The process of creating a title for distribution. It combines the creative and technical aspects of the process.

bandwidth   A measure of the amount of data, or its rate of transfer. A modem may allow transfer of data at a rate of 56.6 kbps (thousand bits per second).

bitmap   A way of representing images for the computer. It is essentially the pattern of dots that make up a picture and can be manipulated by a computer. Bitmaps are generally large files because each dot of the image is represented by a number. They are also prone to "jaggies"—jagged edges caused by enlarging the bitmaps so that lines develop a "stair step" look when the extra dots are added for the enlargement.

bookmarks   A list of favorite or otherwise commonly used web addresses that is semipermanently retained in the browser's bookmark menu for user retrieval.

Boolean search   A type of search system using the words "and," "or," "not," and so on to define the search request. Results require exact matches of words in the request with words in the database text.

browser   A computer program used to navigate the World Wide Web and display its content.

byte   An 8-bit binary word used as a single unit to store and retrieve data.

call-out   A label added to a graphics figure.

CD-ROM   Any compact disc with data on it. Technically, an audio compact disc is a CD-ROM, but the term is generally used to mean any non-audio compact disc. More currently, the term tends to be used to denote compact discs containing data that can be used in a computer system.

CD-ROM drive   A device that reads data from CD-ROM discs into a computer.

check box   a graphic box that can be selected when the user clicks on it to select the term with which it is connected. Check boxes are usually found next to each item in a list of terms. Unlike radio buttons, more than one check box can be selected within a list.

codec Compression/decompression. Algorithms that compress files to make them smaller for faster transmission, then decompress them for playback usually used for audio and video transmission. See *compression*.

compact disc A 5.25" plastic disc with a reflective surface on one side that can be encoded and read with a laser beam. Used without any further description, the term generally means the audio compact disc developed and promoted by Philips and Sony. The compact disc is an international standard for distribution of prerecorded audio.

compression A technique for reducing the amount of data needed to store digital information. Compression is especially useful and usually essential for the storage of large amounts of pictures and video. There are two types of compression: (1) lossy compression achieves its data reduction by selectively leaving out some of the information; and (2) lossless compression uses all of the original information, so there is no reduction in quality when the compressed information is decompressed.

concept search An advanced search system that allows search requests to be phrased in ideas and concepts that do not require exact word matches in the text.

cursor A movable pointer symbol that is on the screen and is used to locate the current screen position for the user. In interactive media, the cursor is used to point to a word, picture, or symbol in order to indicate a choice or to access a hyperlink.

database A library of related information, which can be accessed electronically through a computer or similar device.

digital In a form capable of being processed by a computer. Technically, data converted to ones and zeros—the only type of information a computer can process.

digitize To convert raw assets into digital form.

disc A flat, plastic, circular device containing digital information that is stored optically and can be read by a laser. Often refers to a CD-audio disc.

discoverable   The ability to find a feature or asset in a new media title.

disk   A flat, circular device coated with magnetic material that can be recorded and read by a magnetic head in a computer. Film-based floppy disks can be removed from the computer and transported and stored separately. Metal-based hard disks usually are permanently attached to and remain inside the computer. Hard disks can store much more than floppy disks.

DOS (Disk Operating System)   The essential operating system of PCs, developed by Microsoft for IBM. When the system was sold with an IBM PC, it was called PC-DOS. When it was sold on other computers or by itself, it was called MS-DOS. The computers based on the Intel 8088, 8086, 80286, 80383, 80486, Pentium, and others in that family plus DOS constitute the PC platform.

drag and drop   The process of selecting an object (text or graphic), moving it to another location on the screen, and releasing it onto another object for any type of processing or regrouping.

drilling down   The process of using hyperlinks to move through an information structure. The advantage to this type of navigation is that it presents a neatly organized hierarchy of information to the user.

drop-down field   An input field in which a pre-existing list of possible selections drops down when the user points to it with the cursor. The user can then select an item from the list.

DVD-ROM   An optical disc format providing large-storage capacity for data and other computer applications.

ebook   Any form of electronic book in which the contents are stored and played back digitally.

encoding   Converting information to a digital format capable of being used by a particular system.

FAQ (Frequently Asked Questions, pronounced "fak")   A file containing background information on a topic, originally used in newsgroups.

floppy disk   A magnetic disk (usually 3.5" or 5.25" in diameter) that can store data and can be removed and transported to another computer that uses the same operating system. Floppies can store less information than most hard disks, but they are removable and can be used as a means of distributing information or programs.

FTP (File Transfer Protocol)   An original Internet protocol used to transfer data files in an noninteractive fashion.

GIF (Graphics Interchange Format)   A graphics format first devised for the CompuServe system, now widely used in Web images.

GUI (Graphical User Interface)   Icon-based display programs promoting simple mouse-driven, point and click use. Often pronounced "gooie."

hard disk (hard drive)   A large-capacity magnetic storage device used in computers. Data recorded on a hard disk remains there until erased or overwritten by other data. Hard disks usually are nonremovable inside the computer.

hardware   All of the components of the physical computer or machine. The processor, the memory chips, the storage devices, and the monitor are all hardware.

home page   The first and main document that appears on a Web site, often directing the user to subsequent pages.

host   A main computer used to control communications.

hot spot   A place on the screen (word, phrase, picture, or graphic design) that contains a hyperlink. The hot spot can be linked to text elsewhere in the ebook, or it can trigger playback of an audio or video clip, among many other things.

HTML (Hypertext Markup Language)   The language used to code text files, primarily used for documents found on the Web.

HTTP (HyperText Transfer Protocol)   An international standard transmission protocol used for Web files.

hyperlink (hot link)   A link between two related points in a database. The user can point with a cursor to one link, and by pressing a button while the cursor is positioned over the first link, access the second link.

hypermedia   Multimedia that is dynamically interconnected by hyperlinks.

hypertext   Text that uses links to dynamically connect to other, often elaborating, text.

iadverb   An adverb as used in an interactive title.

inoun   An noun as used in an interactive title.

interactive   Media that dynamically responds to the user. Interactive media are connected via a system of links. These links respond to the user's pointing with a cursor and pressing one or more buttons on a cursor controller.

Internet   A series of interconnected networks with local, regional, and national networks, using the same telecommunications protocol (TCP/IP). Provides e-mail, remote login, and file transfer. The Web is communicated via the Internet.

Internet address   A unique numeric address that identifies a computer connected to the Internet.

intranet   A computer network that is used for internal (as opposed to external) Internet communication.

iprep   A preposition as used in an interactive title.

iverb   A verb as used in an interactive title.

Java   A cross-platform programming language developed and promoted by Sun Microsystems for sending programs called "applets" over the Internet. These applets are sent in partially compiled form and are then fully compiled by the user's browser. In this way, complex programs can be sent quickly over the Internet, and they can add a wide variety of functionality to the user's computer. Its proponents envision a computer user renting programs such as word processors from online vendors.

JPEG (Joint Photographic Experts Group)   An image file format allowing different levels of file compression.

linear   A medium that runs from beginning to end and is not designed for user manipulation (except stopping and starting). Television, movies, live theater, video and audio tape, and to a lesser degree records and compact discs are all examples of linear media. It can be argued that individual tracks on records and compact discs can be played in any order, but generally they are programmed to be played sequentially. Some compact disc players have features that randomly shuffle the order of tracks automatically. This makes compact discs a slightly less linear medium than a traditional vinyl disc.

link   A hypertext path connecting one part of documents or different documents.

menu   A text or graphic screen that lists choices for the user, which can be selected by pointing with the cursor and pressing a button.

MIME (Multipurpose Internet Mail Extensions)   Formats used to send binary files as email or attach files to email. Hypermedia formats in general.

mirror site   A secondary Web or FTP site with identical content to a primary site. Used to lessen traffic on the primary site.

Mosaic   The first hypermedia browser program (now rarely used) developed to navigate the Internet.

MPEG (Motion Picture Experts Group)   A variety of standards used to data-compress audio and video files.

multimedia   A medium which combines text, audio, and video in an interactive product or service.

new media   Any electronic media employing interactivity for its means of expression.

nonlinear   Material authored in a way to promote nonsequential access to the contents.

OCR   (Optical Character Recognition) A computer program which translates an image of text into editable ASCII coded text.

online   A service which provides access to a database over telephone lines or broadcast.

operating system   The software which, when run on a computer, constitutes the platform. It is the essential software which runs all the other (application) software.

optical media   Any of the media which are designed to be written and read by a laser. These include compact discs, CD-ROM, CD-i, and laser discs.

OS (Operating system)   The software which, when run on a computer, constitutes the platform. It is the essential software which runs all the other (application) software.

PC (Personal Computer)   Also used to denote any personal computer which is based on the Intel 8086, 8088, 80286, 80386, i486, Pentium, or compatible chips. These are often referred to as IBM clones. Most often used to differentiate all of these machines from machines made by Apple Computer and others.

platform   The combination of hardware and operating system software which defines an installed base for potential users of a given piece of software.

radio button   A method of selecting one from several items in a list. When a selection from the list is made, any previous selection is canceled. Named for old style radio station selection buttons which forced previously selected station buttons to pop out when a new one was selected. See *check box*.

RAM (Random-Access Memory)   The memory inside any computer or computer device which disappears when the device is turned off. Data stored in RAM is held there temporarily while it is stored, manipulated, or read by the user. Data in RAM is lost when the power of the computer is turned off.

rollover   An area of the computer screen which reveals additional information when the cursor enters its boundary. Also, the visual change in an area of the screen when the cursor enters its boundary indicating that some further action is possible if the user then clicks on it.

ROM (Read-Only Memory)   Information that is permanently part of the structure of the hardware. It is usually stored in a chip. It cannot be modified or overwritten and it exists when the power to the computer is shut off.

screen metaphor   A graphical environment, such as an art museum, used as a physically realistic virtual backdrop for organizing the content of a title.

search engine   The computer program that allows the location and retrieval of information in a database.

server   A computer connected to a network and used to provide services such as holding a database or Web page, or directing email.

SGML (Standard Generalized Markup Language)   A software protocol developed to provide a standard way to format documents so that they could be searched more easily by search engines. Precursor to HTML.

software   Usually this refers to computer programs, but in the context of electronic publishing, it refers to any material which is playable on hardware. In practical terms this means the published material in salable form. Software for a VCR is a videocassette, for example. We've heard it said that software for a microwave oven is food.

tag   Any of many code strings embedded in an HTML document which determine graphical layout, hyperlinks, and embedded objects such as ActiveX or Java-written applets, or multimedia file downloading and opening.

TCP/IP (Transmission Control Protocol/Internet Protocol)   A set of protocols that standardize data transfer between computers connected to the Internet.

TIFF (Tagged Image File Format)   A format used to store image files; not compressed, and may contain multiple images.

title   Any electronic work, for either CD-ROM or online distribution, that employs new media.

UNIX   An operating system used by many network computers.

URL (Uniform Resource Locator)   An address describing a specific document on the web. Sometimes pronounced "earl."

USENET   A large number of globally available newsgroups, adhering to a set of rules, in which users may post and read text, graphics, etc.

user   The human who navigates an interactive title or use a software program.

.wav   A format used to store audio files.

Web (World Wide Web, WWW)   *See World Wide Web.*

Web browser   A software program used to access the Web and use hyperlinks to move from site to site. Also used in conjunction with software plug-in programs to listen to audio files, view video programs, and interact with other assets on Web sites. Often, browsers from Netscape and Microsoft are used.

Web server   A computer holding Web pages and used to distribute them over a network.

Web site   A collection of interlinked files and documents written with HTML and available on the Internet.

Windows   A graphical, user-friendly operating system used in most computers with Intel-made CPUs.

World Wide Web ("the Web," WWW)   The worldwide network of computers and documents that uses HTML markup language.

Index